MADE UP

ArtCenter Graduate Press

Imprint

EDITORS
Tim Durfee
Mimi Zeiger

GRAPHIC DESIGN
Benjamin Critton Art Dept.

EXECUTIVE PRODUCER
Anne Burdick,
MDP Chair

COPY EDITOR
Braulio Agnese

RESEARCHERS
Kyra Lunenfeld
Jessica Lee

PRINTING
American Foothill

SPECIAL THANKS
Brian Roettinger

MADE UP
Design's Fictions

ArtCenter College of Design /
Media Design Practices

☐   Media
      Design
      Practices

©   ArtCenter Graduate Press
      2017

      Actar Publishers
      New York, Barcelona

☐   artcenter.edu/mdp
☐   actar.com

ISBN
978–1–5323–4788–7

A CIP catalogue record for this
book is available from Library of
Congress, Washington, DC, USA.

DISTRIBUTION
Actar D, Inc.

New York
440 Park Ave South
17th Floor
New York, NY 10016
United States

T   +1 212 966 2207
E   salesnewyork@actar-d.com

Barcelona
Roca i Batlle 2–4
08023 Barcelona
Spain

T   +34 933 282 183
E   eurosales@actar-d.com

Made Up

4 – 5	FOREWORD / FORWARD	Anne Burdick
6 – 9	INTRODUCTION	Mimi Zeiger
10 – 15	ASPIRANTS TO REALITY Possible Essays on the Made Up	Tim Durfee
18 – 26	SYMPOSIUM KEYNOTE January 29, 2011	Bruce Sterling
27	PROPS MAKE THE FUTURE	Julian Bleecker
28 – 33	THE FUTURE NEVER GETS OLD On Julian Bleecker	Emmet Byrne + Susannah Schouweiler
34 – 37	META-METAHAVEN	Benjamin H. Bratton + Metahaven
38 – 40	STORIED STOREYS Architecture's Real Fictions	Sam Jacob
41 – 42	SYMPOSIUM KEYNOTE January 29, 2011	Fiona Raby
43	PLASTIC FUTURES MARKETS	Benjamin H. Bratton
44 – 48	DREAMING TOGETHER	Stuart Candy
49 – 54	UNSOLVING THE CITY	Geoff Manaugh + China Miéville
55	EXPANSIONARY TALES	Geoff Manaugh
56	BESPOKE FUTURES	Peter Lunenfeld
57 – 58	GUISES OF THE CASTLE	m-a-u-s-e-r
59 – 66	DEAD RECKONING The Endless Rediscovery of America	Norman M. Klein
67 – 80	EXCERPTS FROM OFFICE POLICY	MOS
81 – 93	THE EXPEDITER	Tom Marble
94 – 101	RAINY SEA	Keith Mitnick
104	Contributor Biographies	Eds.

FOREWORD

Anne
Burdick

MDP
Chair

Summer
2017

Here in Pasadena, at the edge of Los Angeles, on the brink of the Pacific, daily life is a concoction of future and fiction. One morning, I met a Trader Joe's shopper who was literally operating on Martian time: He's a Mars Rover driver from NASA's Jet Propulsion Lab just up the street. At least once a month, my local bodega becomes a "crime scene" for a *telenovela* that's been running for decades. When I stream HBO, I see my real-life neighbor, but she's someone else, in another time and place entirely. ■ It's a fitting setting, then, for a graduate design program intent upon pushing the boundaries of long-standing disciplines to ask the question: What else is possible? How else might the world be? What other worlds can we imagine? How far can we stretch the boundaries of design? ■ Playing at the crossroads of diverse disciplines, the faculty and students of the Media Design Practices program (MDP) have been asking these questions since the mid-nineties. Our mission has always been to interrogate norms and to push into the unknown. To do otherwise would be to waste the promise of graduate school and to ignore that concoction of future and fiction that defines our place and time. ■ This book reminds us of the MDP's forward-looking history and marks

FORWARD

a significant moment when leading voices and projects were coalescing into an all-out movement, before the term speculative design was on everyone's lips. *Made Up: Design's Fictions* — a look at what happens when design and fiction are conjoined — began in 2010 with a series of readings, screenings, and talks led by core faculty member Tim Durfee. Then, in 2011, the program staged an exhibition that was radically inclusive of practices that seldom occupy the same space physically or conceptually. Projects were installed within *The Rather Large Array*, an experiment in architecture and media. ■ For the last five years, our curriculum has followed two tracks, Lab and Field, encouraging plurality, discord, and the collision of worlds. One aim of the *Made Up* exhibition was to put the new ideas that were emerging from this curriculum in direct dialogue with the field at large. ■ In 2017, as we publish *Made Up: Design's Fictions*, a retrospective look at what might be, our program's mission remains the same — to question norms and imagine differently — but how we go about doing that and what we will call it next is TBD. The writings in this book are a reminder that we have always been most comfortable being on the edge of something that has yet to be fully defined. ■

Mimi Zeiger
2017

INTRODUCTION

A few years before "fake news" entered our cultural lexicon, ArtCenter's Media Design Practices MFA program began a conversation about lies, fantasies, and other un-real scenarios. *Made Up: Design's Fictions*, an exhibition and series of public lectures curated by architect and ArtCenter faculty member Tim Durfee with Haelim Paek, opened to the public in late January 2011 in the Wind Tunnel Gallery. A group show of international established and emergent practices, the exhibition questioned the role of design in what was then the budding discourse of "design fiction." ■ The term, indebted to the work of both artist and technologist Julian Bleecker and science fiction novelist Bruce Sterling, represents a broad category of critical design that includes overlapping interests in science fiction, world building, spec-ulation, and futuring. As an exhibition and a volume of texts, *Made Up: Design's Fictions* draws from this plu-rality and is hesitant to privilege any one claim. ■ Still, it was at the *Made Up* symposium that Sterling first laid out some of his initial thoughts on design fiction and, as you'll read in the transcription of his keynote address, suggested that it is "the deliberate use of diegetic prototypes to suspend disbelief about change." With that, Sterling gives us three working param-eters: objects (critical, imaginary, or otherwise), belief (in an alternate or parallel reality), and time (the idea that change is a half-step removed from our now). Fiona Raby presented a second keynote in which she used the work of her London-based design studio Dunne & Raby to illustrate the use of objects — prototypes or, in her term "functional fictions" — to counter certain modernist hang-ups and, perhaps, liberate design from any necessity to perform usefulness. ■ As for belief, this collection of texts asks the reader to wade in deeper and deeper. And deeper. The loose three-part structure reflects this immersion. Definitions and more didactic discussions of design fiction slip into enactments of the theme and finally give way to full-blown narratives. ■ And what about time? It bears mentioning that this book has taken its time to manifest. A hazard and a benefit of a long gestation is that it allows for changes to and augmentations of the original premise. A future in 2011 or 2013 (when a second round of textual materials were commissioned) means something different in 2017. We've come to embrace the awkward diachronics of pasts, presents, and futures. ■ Design culture, like society itself, is subject to acceleration. In the intervening years since Sterling and Raby took the stage in Pasadena, design fiction has rapidly matured into an established area of practice. Tastes and interests have grown and shifted as ideas are shared across digital platforms. So, while the big "What if?" questions of early design fiction could seem naïve in retrospect — the musings of designers and thinkers still feeling the after-effects of the global economic downturn and a relative lack of paid work — the themes of *Made Up* seem more relevant now than ever. As if the passing of time has once again made strange our understandings of design. ■

ASPIRANTS TO REALITY

Possible Essays on
the Made Up

MADE UP

In *Mimesis*, Erich Auerbach argues that Western literature emerged from two primary modes of writing: the rhetorical tradition (as found in Homer) of unambiguous description of the foreground and the present, and the realism (in the sense of emotional realism) of the Bible, that communicates with multiplicities of meaning, implications of the unexpressed, and a "preoccupation with the problematic." In *The Odyssey*, a goat on the battlefield is just a goat. In the realist tradition however, significance — and a form of emotional familiarity — is implied by the very deliberateness of the goat's presence. It is made up, and through that willful act, made more real.

Architecture and design are borne of similar contradictions. They begin as dreams, become incarnate as facts — only to be rewritten as fictions as their inexplicit meanings yield to new purposes and desires. There can be no single account for this phenomenon, or why it matters. There are, however, many accounts. All possible, though, of course, all made up.

GET REAL

When does something become real? A drawing for an unbuilt building is merely a scheme, but if someone commissions the building, or simply buys the drawing, it becomes economically real. If an agency approves the project for construction, then it becomes legally real. A building also becomes real if it is built, but it won't be for the first time.

Like identifying signal from noise, determining which form reality takes depends on the context and purpose. What, really, distinguishes a map from an encyclopedia, a novel from a game, a social network from a movie, or a building from a city? Each represents a different set of arrangements — according to certain values and needs — along a shared continuum of the world's matter and information. Lemons need only to serve a different reality to be lemonade.

REALITY is a CONTEST

The story of everything? Some realities yield to others. Light, matter, life, politics, commerce, relationships, thoughts, dreams — all exist in one form at the expense of another possible form.

Our happiness — indeed, our existence — is made more secure by being able to predict or influence what realities will prevail. Prediction and persuading both require speculation. Stories appeal to us not because they are untrue, but rather because they might be true, and therefore provide useful information or ideas in our navigation through eventual, possible, realities.

If the present could be thought of as a stationary line crossing an intricate mesh of vectors shooting across time — some ancient, some new, some yet to be — then stories are a form of reality attached, as it were, to one of these passing vectors: possible pasts, possible presents, possible futures — all arrows in the epic battle for reality (in 3D, both screens!).

☐ *Crashing into horizons, on the brink of success! Hurrah! Success which was survival gone too far.*
— "All the Things That Go to Make Heaven and Earth"
A.C. Newman
The New Pornographers

ACROSS the MULTIVERSE

Depending on who you ask, any one thing can be countless other things. The criminal looks for weaknesses, the detective for clues, the developer for undervalue, the seller for overvalue, the politician for approval, the doctor for symptoms, the comedian for ironies. For each thing, countless cosmologies. This is a type of multiverse.

Fiction (but also design and architecture) creates provisional realities for others to occupy. It conjures artifacts from our otherwise insular worlds to possibly be recognized by someone else as familiar. Indeed, for all of David Foster Wallace's complexity as a novelist of ideas, literature was ultimately, for him, "to make us feel less alone." Through making we pilot across the multiverse of subjectivities.

GUEST LIST

Social utopians, Ballardian dystopians, techno-fetishists, socio-sexual-racial liberation futurists, heroic neo-Moderns, art world outsiders, art world insiders, progressive policy wonks, reactionary policy doctors, pure science materialists, agents of The Singularity, burners, sci-fi enthusiasts, lit-major poets, art-smart ironic pranksters, earnest engineers, casual gamers, hardcore gamers, game designers, tinker-y maker-y doodlers, conspiracy theorists, techno-formalist fabulists, eco-doomsday prophets, silicon valley dot com opportunists, steam punks, S.T.E.A.M. punks, actors, authors, crypto-mystic-coders, futures traders, future traders, trippy nightmare mystics, lab-coated empiricists, dreamy aesthetes, field gear and gadget freaks … .

IN YOUR DREAMS

To live is to want: love, health, a decent parking spot. In making, we attempt to replace the phantom world of our desires with solid stuff. Making preempts the dream, lost.

☐ *Preemptive nostalgia of the possible but doubtful.*
— "Paper Hearts"
Yoni Wolf
WHY?

DESIGN MAKES PROBLEMS

It started at a client lunch meeting, years ago. "That will be no problem at all," you said, but of course it was a problem. It was THE problem. What should this thing be? What alchemy of experience, knowledge, and information will produce the idea to make the thing? What arrangement of materials, language, technology will produce the thing? You signed the bill and exited into the bleached daylight of East Hollywood, having created seventeen new problems. Design just makes more problems.

FORM as FICTION

In a context of pragmatic and rational design, willful form can be understood as a type of fiction: straying from the utilitarian script to serve an expressive agenda. However, to the degree that every form of design has an intrinsic utilitarian script, today there are fewer and fewer necessary accommodations to affect form.
Additionally, the expanding connectedness of everything is making it less possible to think of objects as having qualities unique to themselves, rather than as parts of the systems within which they exist. Thus liberated from any vestigial determinants to shape, even the

most objective form will go looking for alternate determining logics, alternate narratives.
But what, after all, is "objective form"? Often, that is a status reserved for pure geometry: the infinitely scalable relational truth of the universe. The form of nature itself: the "real." Geometry is, however, an unbuildable ideal. It is a representational instrument whose claims to objectivity are weakened by the very ideological weight of those who declare its mystical virtuousness. Geometry, too, is itself a type of fiction.

PYRAMID SCHEMES

Economies rise and fall in a strange cycle of speculation. Financial and property speculators dream in the margins and rounding errors of the economy to great profit, which inevitable over-exuberance eventually collapses. Political, social, and cultural speculators then dream of alternatives to the world made by the previous crew of speculators. The eventual recovery restores the system. Then, seeing an opportunity, the financial and property speculators resume their dreaming.

n.b.
Those who speculate, and succeed, are called visionaries. Those who speculate, and fail, are called speculators.

☐ *A landmark which commands the world and is looked upon by the world with respect. [It will] make one intoxicated, as if he were enjoying himself in the fabulous heaven.*

— from developer's press release for the 18-million-square-foot New Century Global Centre in Chengdu, China, the world's largest building.

☐ *There are no unbuildable buildings, only unbuilt ones.*
— Etienne-Louis Boullée

WORLD, BUILDING

Real things and spaces are stage-craft for plays to be written by their users. They eventually become prompts for the ideas, fantasies, histories, beliefs, fears, and halluci-nations that comprise a culture. But what about living in narrative worlds as users, with our own agendas? Turning left at the corner, where the writer turned right ... .

V.R. MODERNISM

Since the declaration of an International Style, modernism has moved us ever further from the realities of the vernacular: the rootedness of things in place and culture. Although some of the postmodernisms attempted a reconnection, it was already too late: irrelevant (or relevant to something else), and in quotes. "Super," and other prefixes attempt to describe a still further detached modernism — exemplified by the non-places of globalism's infrastructure: airports and rootless branded environ-ments. Even so, many historical styles were merely appropriations of vernacular approaches to fulfill social or cultural fantasies. Hellenic

details spoke of democratic values. Sundry non-Western styles evoked Romantic visions of travel or con-quest. With globalization, will there ever again be a vernacular that is "authentic"? Has economic expe-diency rendered style as willful, so even the most regional style (in that region itself) is necessarily exotic? And what is next in this unrelent-ing trajectory away from history, away from connections to place, away from connections to time? Is design's eventual departure from reality entirely — a virtual-real — the final stage of the modern project?

HOST

Software transmits values: artificial intelligence systems propagate the biases of their coders; cinematic creatures and skyscrapers are made with the same digital tools; first per-son shooters train both gamers and soldiers. These monsters, latent deep in the code, awaken surreptitiously in cities and homes around the world.

DIACHRONICLES

To design something is to create a provisional future. A small piece of time travel. What does it mean to design something new, but for the past? What can this tell us about where we are now?

Predictive algorithms analyze everything about us and construct models that asymptotically, tanta-lizingly, terrifyingly approach per-fection. New relationships to the present and the past will gradually emerge when all people, places, and things have their entire histo-ries completely captured. Nothing forgotten, reality will be free to drift from the present, through the associative realities of countless linked datasets. Similar to the way mathematicians imagine glimpses of higher dimensions as "shadows" projected into our 3D world, perhaps we will be able to imagine shadows of the future in our present. Eventually, an entire landscape of algorithmically offered shadows, onto which we plan the future of our species, our cities, our world.

SPOCK'S FLIP-PHONE

Visions of the future entertain, inspire, then become a part of our collective memory. We make the world from our memory of those futures.

FUTURE, NEVER in STYLE

Sitting at the table with the group, Future looks ridiculous in his tasteless jacket and ridiculous hat. He looks around the room — all versions of his former self — confidently smiling and enjoying their cigarettes. He'll never fit in.

MADE BELIEF

Objects, media, and spaces can embody belief systems in ways more profound than written language, yet their enduring power is often underestimated. Who says a wall has to functionally work to actually divide? Ideologies beget form. Form can be the executioner or the savior. Or maybe just be the thing that really ties the room together.

LET A HUNDRED OVERPRICED, ORGANIC, HYPOALLERGENIC, CONFLICT-FREE FLOWERS BLOOM

There is renewed call for design to solve the world's challenges. However, many of the tools we use to address the problems of the future created the problems of the present. As we attempt to save continents from drought, address all physical impairments, cure global poverty, can we be certain our real purpose is not merely to assure the unfortunates who live by the Amazon can also shop on Amazon?

BARK v. BITE

She sits in the boardroom, approving or rejecting proposed defense equipment as the schemes are presented. Eventually, two drawings are brought in — each for a different new jet fighter. She is asked to approve one of these designs for final development, but since the data suggests they will perform equally well, and cost the same, it is not clear how to reach a final decision. There is something about the engine inlet openings being closer together on one of the designs. Is it that predators in the animal kingdom have eyes forward and the eyes of prey are further apart? Avion de chasse, Jagdflugzeuge: the French and German words for fighter planes remind us these are hunters. But is not the actual role of these priceless machines — perhaps above performance itself — deterrence? She finally decides communicating menace is part of the plane's performative mandate, and submits her vote.

The PROTECTIVE NIGHTMARE

We have avoided nuclear apocalypse only through the horrific conclusions of a speculative mortal calculus. As there is no possible empirical knowledge of exactly how global nuclear powers will respond when provoked, we rely on speculative math to suitably haunt those in charge.

In a similar way, climate change requires scientific "dreaming" to predict its potentially irreversible effects. These are challenges that require deliberate, disciplined story-telling. With these existential threats, there can be no "I told you so." It is required of us, therefore, to "tell" better, and faster.

WHAT'S SO FUNNY 'BOUT PEACE, LOVE, and UNDERSTANDING?

Conflicts arise when incompatible realities are required to coexist. Humor, however, requires these forms of confusion — the forces in conflict serve a punchline, not an agenda. Does peace come from getting the joke? New ideas can be absurd, perhaps laughable. Until they are not. Then maybe they become works of genius. (Which is, alas, less funny.)

The ART of the DEAL

Once facts are subject to human perception they are tainted with bias. Even data, once communicated, is subject to selection and emphasis. Is art, then, more honest because its subjectivity is not concealed? Indeed, art's subjectivity is its form of reality: "The lie that tells the truth."

Art has long served critical and radical causes. Today, however, conspiratorialists and reactionaries declare themselves performance artists to protect their hate-filled diatribes from legal accountability. Is this cynical form of political action the ultimate expanded field for art? Where art's inherent confusion of reality and fiction provides the ideal plausible deniability? The art of kleptocracy, the art of hate speech, the art of border walls, the art of war, the art of the deal ... .

PRETENDERS to the THRONE

You put down your pen (on the side it reads: Your business name here). With many essays still to write, you wonder: "Why does this matter now?"

At his private resort, the leader pushes aside martinis and shrimp cocktails to make room for the nuclear launch device, billionaire bros high-five each other as their ruinous pranks accumulate, Internet trolls march into the daylight in surreal cos-plays of hate, drug-resistant diseases spread the globe, polar bears wander into malls and gas stations.

Don't these threatening realities require action that is concrete, tangible, and pragmatic? Isn't this the time for all creative energy to promote the real? Democracy is an algorithm, and good data must go in for good to come out. If the gravest oppression is declaring reality as false, then resistance requires mastery of the made up as well as of the made. We must be both producers and pretenders. Pretenders to warn, pretenders to provoke, pretenders to inspire. Pretenders to new and better realities. ∎

The Rather Large Array
Photo Catherine R.
Wygal + Deanna McClure

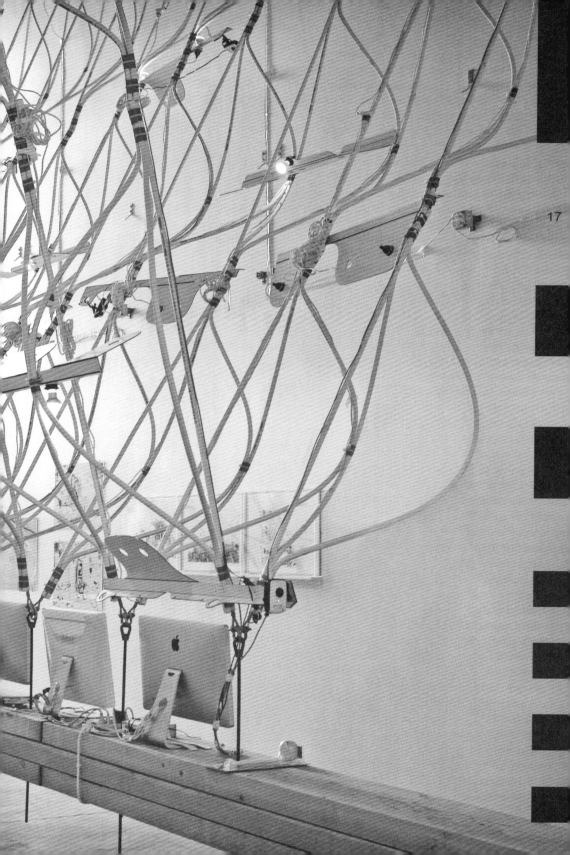

SYMPOSIUM KEYNOTE

January 29, 2011

UP

MADE

People have been talking about design fiction for quite a while now. It's starting to get some texture, so I've come here in order to offer you a formal definition for the first time ever.

So what is design fiction? Design fiction is "the deliberate use of diegetic prototypes to suspend disbelief about change."

What do I mean by "deliberate use"? I mean if you do design fiction, you have to be aware that it is a practice. Other people have done it, and they are doing it now. You have to become aware of its context within the design world. It's not a form of design that is accidentally speculative or critical; it's deliberately so.

Diegetic prototypes are prototypes. They're quite like traditional prototypes of goods and services, except they're "diegetic," which is a term from theater and film criticism. A "diegetic prototype" is showy: It catches the eye of an audience, arouses some futuristic engagement or enthusiasm. Design has clients and users; design fiction has an audience and followers. When you see a diegetic prototype, your reaction is not "Oh, what's that? Can I buy it?" but "Wow" or "What a difference that would make." You may be disturbed by it — or feel that it somehow moves the world in a new direction.

"Suspension of disbelief " is also an important term. This practice is not restricted to the traditional literary methods of suspending disbelief in a reader of fiction. It's about using much wider methods of suspending disbelief in a user, or a viewer, or a participant.

Then there is the term "change". I make no claim that this "change" is good or bad, positive or negative. Design fiction is not an inherently "good" thing to do. It's a set of tools and methods, most of them long known in the design world. "Fiction" can arise from any number of ideological and moral standpoints.

So why is this happening now? What is design fiction, and how does it work? What's so different about it? Well, let's start by trying to define its opposite: design fact. What sure knowledge do we possess about designed objects and services — what do we know that is entirely factual? What is the true and objective nature of goods and services?

What sharp lines can we draw between things that are entirely fact-based and phantom suppositions that are deceptive and fictional?

Well, there is the judgment of history. Some goods and services are dead by now. They no longer arouse any human passions. They have no champion groups eager to valorize or de-valorize them. With mankind's extinct creations we can achieve a certain objectivity. A dead object is no longer evolving, developing, aspiring to become a new-and-improved object. Ripped from daily life, it is stripped of symbolism. We know where it went, where it came from. It is a fossil. Describing fossils is as close as we can get to a timeless knowledge.

Outside the realm of the dead, living objects drift, shade-by-shade, step-by-step, into the speculative. It is never a realm of sharp black-and-white divisions; there are always tints of human assumption and pretense.

Let's consider engineering specifications, patents, technical blueprints, and so forth. These careful documents allegedly allow us to accurately build or manufacture one of these objects. It's surprising how much these official documents vary from the actual goods and services that become available in real life. Patents frequently stretch the truth in the hope of legal and financial gain. However, their purpose is to be accurate. They're commonly assumed to be accurate. At least, they're certified.

The next layer is one of legal regulations, government protocols. Naturally, a government tries to regulate the designed objects within its sovereignty, and it needs legal description in order to sue for certain misdeeds. Objects and services rather often end up in a court of law. The legal system tries to separate good intent from bad intent, to find justice in truth, and so forth.

However, we all know that the legal system fudges on occasion. Legal argument is incessant. That which is found legally true is not necessarily absolutely true. One nation's legal system doesn't agree with another's. Ask various nations who invented the airplane, the radio, the television, or the telephone. They're all very sincere.

Then there's design criticism and scholarly assessments. Here certain people, who commonly don't have a lot of skin in the real-world design game, are trying to make wise assessments about designed goods and services. Chairs, for instance. We've all seen books which divide chairs up, quite neatly, into schools of chairmaking: materials, regions, theories, sizes, colors, arcs of historical development, and so on. Do these learned books agree with one another about chairs? No, they don't. There are quarrels among design critics. Scholars fight about things. The less that is apparently at stake, the more scholars are eager to quarrel over it.

Another stage in this drift toward fiction: product reviews and user feedback. Perhaps you feel the need of a chair, so you go online to see what people say about chairs. At this point we are venturing into fandom and popular folk myth. Fierce devotees of turn-of-the-century steamed bentwood chairs. High-tech elitists insisting on lightweight titanium chairs. User feedback is full of crazy trolls: outright lunatics who hate the chairs, who want to sue the manufacturer and seller, who will claim that the chair murdered a child. The Internet is like that.

Instruction manuals. We've all seen them. They may seem very dry, very factual, truthful, but how many times have you received an instruction manual, only to find that it has little to do with the object at hand? Commonly, reading the instruction manual is a last-ditch effort by the user. There's a lot of rhetoric in them: neatly numbered stages, one, two, three, four, five. How rarely these coincide with what actually happens to the builder.

Plans and schematics. Business strategies. Suppose that I'm in the business. I'm making these designed things for a living. I'm trying to tell my colleagues what I'm doing. We've got internal white papers, we're describing the objects and the service within the enterprise. Are these truthful documents? Or are they mostly documents meant for internal political purposes?

One can read these things, or try writing them. I've seen a lot of internal business communications. Even within one company, they're commonly rhetorical. Engineering and marketing may be quarreling. Public relations hates the web people. These internal communications are intended to persuade.

Let's talk about design pitches. Are those factual? I'm a designer; I'm going to your company; I need to explain to your company brass why it is that you should make industrial products in my way. I had better be persuasive, and even dramatic, given that I'm a passing outsider in your company, and I want you to hire me.

I'm going to transform your product line — then I'm going to leave. To win your trust, I had better be a rather glamorous and persuasive figure. I'm a designer. If I simply show my accountancy skills in your internal bean counting, I won't get hired.

Much better that I should be Henry Dreyfuss: businesslike, but dressed in a unique brown suit, and fully prepared with an excellent, unorthodox elevator pitch. I need to have — not exactly "fiction" — but I need to have a well-prepared presentation with a certain amount of calculated theatricality.

I need to move conservative people off the dime because I'm asking them to spend, let's say, $10 million to reformat their industrial production line. I don't have a lot of time to make my point. I don't want to spend much time cajoling the irrelevant board of directors. To design proper objects and services, I mostly want to talk to the marketers, the engineers, and the manufacturers. Getting the bosses to sign off on the project is more or less a presentation skill.

What comes next? Brand management. And what is that? How much persuasion and fictionality is involved in brand management?

Heaps!

Before the idea of brand management was invented, one might simply remark, "You know, we'd better not do that. That's unethical and dishonorable, and it would make us look bad."

But once I have brand management, I rejoice in a much broader approach. I am keenly aware of the thought leaders, opinion makers, and publicity leaders in my arena. I have named and numbered the media outlets I can exploit. I know where to place my messages, where to listen, how to twist the discourse in my direction — how to maneuver myself into another presentational space, where my brand escapes damage and is enhanced with a new demographic. I can track all these things now. I manage the brand.

And then there's design fiction, which I think is quite close to brand management in its innate degree of fictionality. Design fiction means the use, as I said, of diegetic prototypes to suspend disbelief about change.

"Diegetic prototypes" are not "brands," but they are similarly immaterial. In design fiction, you're creating imaginary objects. You're creating "theory objects," conversation pieces that are intended to provoke debate. Design fictions are intended to move people away from fixed idea, to loosen their credulity. They're intended to disturb, to persuade, to get people to break loose, to move outside the box.

You are "suspending disbelief" — but that is an ethical choice. You can also choose to lie, to lunge for belief and try to illegitimately keep it. When you lie, you promulgate fictions about speculative goods and services that you know are untrue. This is vaporware. Vaporware is a fear, uncertainty, and doubt campaign.

If you intensify design fiction by hiring a design fiction cynic and mercenary, he will make vaporware. He will cloud the customer's eyes with intentional deceit in order to make money or to preserve or extend market share: "Our company intends to do this! We're going to bring this product out, and it's going to be like Company A's product, only better and cheaper. So you'd better not buy theirs — you had better wait a couple of quarters until ours is available."

This is a deliberate inculcation. "You could buy our competitor's product — but what if you got into a lot of trouble? Does the competitor's product really work at all? Why don't you succumb to fear, delay, hold off? Don't give them the money now, give us that money later." Companies have been destroyed by powerful, persuasive fictions of this kind. Not just inconvenienced, but destroyed by fictions and deliberately empty promises. Vaporware is powerful.

Then there are parodies, jokes, and whimsy. These are akin to design fictions, but they are played for laughs and are lighter in spirit. Nobody is deceived or harmed by them — the deceit lasts only until the audience gets the joke. Rube Goldberg devices; Heath Robinson devices; the Maywa Denki interventions; Chindogu, which are un-useless objects; wacky Internet-meme gadget knick-knacks. There's a long and honorable tradition of parody and satire in design and technology.

These funny, high-spirited things are not Design Fiction. There is nothing wrong or bad about them, but they're not a form of design, they're a form of comedy.

It's possible to get much more fictional than Design Fiction. Fraudulent commercial advertising, for instance. Let's say that I'm not speculating or designing, I'm just plain lying. I've just decided to deceive you and cheat you because I have bad intent. I'm trying to get you to buy the damn thing, although it's no good, and I know it. I needed the money. I hired certain people, we made it look good. We hired a lot of media and we yelled at you: "It makes you healthy"; "Your kids will love you"; "Buy this, a pretty girl will embrace you." There's tons of this rubbish. Everybody knows how it's done.

Some designed objects are lies in themselves. They're fake products, product forgeries. This was a real, successful, valuable product, and people really wanted it — but I'm a crook. I've decided to make a false one. My fake one costs a lot less, it falls apart, it harms you, it's made of toxic substances. I don't care. I needed the money. I'm a forger. I'm a deceiver.

This is a huge industry. This deceit is easy to perform. It's easy to sell, and it's easy to market. Fake products are all over Internet retail channels. They're all over peer-to-peer services. They're outside legal channels of distribution. Black marketeers are opening car trunks all over the world, bringing out tons of these fake products. Some of these fakes are made by the very same companies that make the real products.

We have megatons of real-world, marketable products that are fictional lies. It's naïve to think that there are certain designed products that are real, while others are mere fictions. There are extensive borderlands here. Effective design fictions are created by designers who know where to step in these shadows.

Design fiction has an important school called "experiential futurity" — a design fiction *Gesamtkunstwerk*, the Design Fiction as total-work-of-art. In "experiential futurity," the designer creates an immersive experience, an apparent future situation with many diegetic prototypes, or even scripted diegetic behaviors. It's design fiction as little theater, encounter therapy, or a Disney Tomorrowland ride.

But "experiential futurity" can also be pushed well past design fiction into savage hinterlands of unethical deceit. This is a sting, a con game. I convince you, the sucker, that I know an imperial princess who has $4 million. You'll get a million if you sit and listen and play along. These elaborate sting frauds are commonly well rehearsed, involving forged bank documents, alleged government ministers sending you e-mail daily, and so forth. Of course, the evil purpose of these fraudsters is to relieve you of some large sum and then vanish.

There isn't a person in this room who hasn't gotten one of those advance-pay fraud emails. Probably you received hundreds of them. Why does this fiction work? Because it's been crowdsourced by mobs of criminals since the late 1800s.

Street theatre is like design fiction. By using puppets and protest signs, I'm trying to encourage your belief in a potential political change. Another world is possible — look at this puppet! We can overthrow the dictator through acts of political symbolism — look, we've thrown paint at his poster, and we've torn his statue down!

These political street interventions are not design fictions. However, they're often pretty similar in size, duration, and budget. Lynchings in effigy and guerrilla street performances, all the way up to Nuremberg-style mass rallies and Trotsky's propaganda trains. The power of these rituals should not be underestimated — they're not so politically "real" as real governance, but they have a social effect.

Design fictions have some other related activities, such as Internet art interventions. I see a lot of these because I curate electronic art fairs.

Device art can be like a design fiction. Here I'm designing a functional, working object for an artistic purpose, rather than for a commercial or industrial purpose. I imagined it, I designed it, I engineered it, I built it, and it actually functions, but it's there to produce an artistic response from an audience.

Performance art. Scenario gaming. "Real play" services, where we play a role-playing game, but we take it into the streets.

Training drills and simulation exercises can be like design fictions. Let's pretend this building is on fire. Where would you go? That is entirely a postulated future situation. Probably, this building will never burn.

However, it's still a good thing to contemplate. Once you've imagined that this building is on fire, should this building actually be on fire, the chances of your survival go way up. You have wisely speculated about the fire extinguishers and the exits. Good for you.

Black propaganda. Military ruses. These are fictions too, but in deadly earnest. I'm using the whole coercive power of the state to convince you. The "Strategic Defense Initiative": We're using the actor Ronald Reagan to pretend that we can shoot Soviet missiles out of the sky. Any physicist in the world could tell you this is a blatant hoax. It's like believing in Creationism — but the point of this fiction is to make the enemy nervous. Military deceit is used to crush the morale of the enemy, to destroy his will to resist. "My giant vengeance weapons will incinerate you." "We have the binary gas weapon." The history of warfare is full of effective, powerful, successful deceits. It's Design Fiction on a much larger scale.

Then there are blatant delusions. Mankind has thousands of these: perpetual-motion machines; zero-point energy devices. These are diegetic prototypes which will never work. They can't ever work. They're physically impossible. Yet they are always popular. They never go away.

Unbelievable numbers of perpetual-motion machines have been invented. Zero-point energy devices break the second law of thermodynamics, so they're basically perpetual-motion machines. There are legions of these things, reinvented every generation.

People can never rid themselves of delusional, aspirational inventions. They're always humming in the background somewhere.

Impossible sci-fi literary devices, such as time machines. Time machines don't exist. They're technically impossible for ten or twelve excellent physical reasons. But they work very efficiently as fictions because you can use time machines to make all kinds of powerful, emotionally moving, thematic points. Time machines are fiction machines that tell us about historical experience. "I went to the distant future, and look, I brought back this strange blue rose." Or, "I went into the past and I knew who my grandmother really was." These are legitimate things to describe — literarily. It's okay they're not real objects or services. They're metaphors.

Beyond delusional inventions are raw, ancient, dark superstitions. Again, legions of these — and again, all serving powerful emotional purposes.

Quack devices. Medical hoaxes. You are sick, you are miserable and desperate, so eat these magic apricot pits — they'll make you better! When you're in pain and anguish, your belief is easy to suspend. Then I can impose all kinds of objects and services on you, hoaxes that will probably hasten you into the grave. New Age crystals, mojo hands, the Philosopher's Stone, whatever you might swallow.

Some supernatural objects are used by elves and fairies. "I left him a bowl of milk on the doorstep, and now he will bless the cattle." This urge is present at the deepest levels of the human psyche. All children believe such things without question. Our pre-human ancestors probably believed such things. These fictional things will never go away; they will always be with us. They're powerfully suggestive. It's part of human nature to believe in the lucky rabbit's foot or to dread the specter of a leaning ladder. Folk superstitions are ingrained into the psyche. They're part of our mental background noise.

And then — finally — at the very peak of disbelieve-ability, there are wondrously impossible things that we believe through faith. Holy relics. Many, many. The Shroud of Turin, the Ark of the Covenant, the Trident of Shiva, the tooth of Buddha. The more we believe in the one, the less we believe in the other — but in all times and places, there is the most absolute conviction that these supernatural things represent the genuine truth of existence.

That's part of our psyche. We can't rid ourselves of this. It means more to us than any real product or functional device ever will. You can always rid yourself of somebody else's deep spiritual convictions — that's easy — but never your own. The Trident of Shiva may sound a bit exotic, depending on your neighborhood, but when it comes to disbelieving your own massively irrational convictions, you can't bear to live without them. They're the shorthand of the human relationship to reality.

So, in conclusion, what is design fiction doing? Well, it's deliberately creating and using prototypes, imaginary objects, imaginary services — because it knows that what we call "real" is never entire "reality," but a slider bar of various unrealities. Knowing this, design fiction can intervene creatively up and down that scale.

You can do design fiction and write a fake instruction manual. You can use design fiction and do an immersive con job. You can do design fiction and structure it as vaporware. You can structure it as an advertising campaign. It's up to you. Try not to abuse your great powers in the cause of evil.

Any of these things are possible today, due to the fact the barriers of entry into media have crashed. Design fiction has become cheap to do, and although it commonly manifests itself as a viral video, it can take on almost any mediated form. Design fiction is ideal for rioting through Henry Jenkins' *Convergence Culture* as a viral gizmo meme. It can be the magazine article that is picked up by newspaper wire services while at the same time spreading virally through blogs and social media. Design Fiction can become an installation, an intervention, a gallery show — it might even become a Kickstarter project where somebody actually creates, sells, and ships some genuine object.

Design fiction is a native emanation of a network society. That's why it's a new thing in the world. Even cars — the ultimate clunky, multi-ton, big-ticket consumer item — are no longer what they were in the past. Cars were once described and sold mostly through TV ads and magazine spreads, but modern cars provoke all kinds of mediated reactions: word of mouth, peer-to-peer. It's been a long time since a hit car caught the public imagination. That's not about the cars, which are much improved lately. It's all about the mediated buzz machine, which is very different now.

I'm not a designer, I'm a science fiction writer. I know how to write "fiction" that has some design awareness. Importing design thinking into science fiction makes little difference to the science fiction genre. The genre's readers are very accepting and are serenely unbothered by the presence of design in their texts.

Design fiction is not design with science fiction in it; it is design with some of science fiction's ontological awareness that reality is mutable. Design fiction is about that mutability, expressed within a period of genuine mutation.

Belief is ductile. Disbelief is severely ductile. Disbelief is always in suspense. We believe that something may be true about some object, some service, even some grand, global, techno-social situation — but we always sense that we might be disillusioned. We know we're not living in truth. We try for moral certainty, but it always eludes us.

Think of what we've been through.

"Wait — I thought that these cigarettes were calming my nerves, making me thoughtful and serious — but now I realize that cigarettes actually kill me. What a vast and terrible fraud! They told me for 100, 200, 300, 400 years that tobacco was America's greatest crop, a product beloved all over the world! Now I learn that it kills, not just me, but also the children and the cat!"

Was that an easy realization? By no means. It took a vast, deliberate campaign. A massive intervention that, decade after decade, broke people of their cigarette addictions. A colossal intervention that vilified cigarettes and their manufacturers, that increased the cost of cigarettes, that forced cigarette packages to abandon their traditional graphic design elegance and carry dreadful political statements. Through a deliberate, hard-fought policy, modern cigarette packages scream in horror, "This will kill you in slow and dreadful pain. It will kill your wife, and your unborn child is coughing in the womb."

This change was a tremendous effort — but it's an allied effort to the subject of my speech here. The disbelief is always suspended. The suspension is inherent in the human condition. The device will pass away. The situation will pass away. Our society will pass away. At some point in the grave and somber passage of time, we will lose our conviction and our certainty about any possible object or service.

Every design we love today will someday become a dusty relic in the archive of history. It might well be entirely forgotten, for very few people are really interested in those archives. Once you can understand this, design fiction comes pretty easy. It's easy because it's not a matter of whether it's "real" or not — it's a matter of how long it is real.

The time has come for design fiction to get up and walk. It's going into museums, it's going into biennales. What it lacks is an archive and some critical assessment: the good, the bad, and the imaginary. ■

UP

MADE

Julian Bleecker

PROPS MAKE THE FUTURE

If there is anything to be gained from the design fiction practice, it is the prankish optimism that comes from "making things up." Making things up is playful and serious at the same time. It's playful in that one can speculate and imagine without the "yeah, but ..." constraints that often come from the dour sensitivies of way-too-grown-up pragmatists. It's serious because the ideas that are "made up" as little designed fictions — formed into props or little films or speculative objects — are materialized things that hold within them the story of the world they inhabit. There is the kernel of a near future, or a different now, or an un-history that starts the mind reeling at the possibilities of what could be.

When an idea is struck into form, we have learned to accept that as proof — a demonstration that this could be possible. The translation from an idea into its material form begins the proof of possibility. Props help. Things to think with and things to help us imagine what could be.

This is how the world around us is made: by people who imagine what could be and then go forth and make it material. Wheels did not suddenly appear on luggage, but there they are, and it's hard to imagine that it didn't happen sooner.

Playfully, seriously making things up is how the world around us comes to be. Don't sit around and wait. Make up the world you want. Believe it. Tell its story. Inhabit it, and it will become. ■

Emmet Byrne +
Susannah Schouweiler

THE FUTURE NEVER GETS OLD

On Julian Bleecker

In a 2013 issue of *Frieze*, artist Ian Cheng discusses the future of fiction and narrative forms, describing the great "anxiety" of our age: trying to make sense of, or narrativize, a world that is constantly changing at a speed that renders traditionally relatable narratives inadequate. He proposes several qualities a narrative format of the future might possess, including one "that requires its authors to embrace contingency and irreversibly change during its making."[1]

The design process — concepting, prototyping, testing, refining, etc. — might embody this quality, and Julian Bleecker is determined to explore its narrative potential. With its context-dependent, collaborative, networked process, imagining design as a fictional medium brings a number of scenarios to mind. Entire worlds speculated from a single object. Narratives that evolve over time based on external feedback. Summoning the future into existence, one tweak at a time. And this is what Design Fiction can be: a method to summon a future by articulating it through the rigorous process of design, exploiting the stories embedded in every object, and influencing popular culture.

Bleecker is one of Design Fiction's main advocates and a former member of Nokia's Design Strategic Projects studio, as well as a founding partner of the Near Future Laboratory, a collective dedicated to "thinking, making, design, development, and research practice speculating on the near future possibilities for digital worlds." Over the past few years he has been developing the idea of Design Fiction as a practice that explores the symbiotic relationship between science fiction and science fact, bringing together storytelling with technology, art, design, and innovation.

As an attitude, Design Fiction has a lot in common with Critical Design as put forward by designers Anthony Dunne and Fiona Raby. However, where Critical Design offers tangible thought experiments

1   Kari Rittenbach, Focus Interview: Ian
    Cheng, *Frieze*, Issue 155, May 2013.

exploring our personal relationships with products and consumerism — often inhabiting the space of the gallery or academia — Design Fiction appears to be oriented toward the kind of popular imaginary more comfortable in the realm of Hollywood films, best-selling novels, Skymall catalogs, and Internet memes. More explicitly, it tackles the relationship between storytelling, media, and technological progress. It is more concerned with the fog of the feedback loop of the design process itself in all its compromised and cluttered glory — the implications of business models, service design, iterative development, copyright laws, product obsolescence, hacker spaces, focus groups, Amazon Mechanical Turk, etc. — than with the clarity of the pure artifact on a pedestal (or kitchen counter). Design Fiction does not fetishize the object, but instead foregrounds the context, the human rituals attached to a thing, the drama unfolding, the ethical issues raised, the science, and especially the transmission of an idea through popular and mass culture at large.

I've come to understand Design Fiction a bit like the inverse of Mundane Science Fiction, a short-lived but influential sub-genre of science fiction — the Dogme 95 of sci-fi. Proposed by author Geoff Ryman and others, it existed primarily as a manifesto, a provocation to science fiction writers, combining aesthetic ambition and clarity with political / ethical intentions. The manifesto — formatted as a list of rules — challenged authors to put aside the clichés of the genre, to avoid the escapism, and instead create plausible near-future speculations. To write science fiction without relying on impossible ideas such as faster-than-light travel, teleportation, interactions with alien cultures — the typical *Star Trek* fare that makes up what Gary Westfahl calls the "consensus future." A Mundane Science Fiction story utilizes futuristic ideas, but only those that are within the realm of plausibility. As the best science fiction stories are elaborate thought experiments, this manifesto requires the writer to tighten their concept, denying them the use of the typical shortcuts, conceivably resulting in more rigorous and original ideas. Politically, the manifesto suggested that typical galaxy-hopping science fiction operates under the general impression that we can "burn through this planet" and move on to other worlds — an escapist perspective that requires no gesture of responsibility towards the present. Adherents to the mundane assert that there is enough happening here on earth to create the sense of wonder strived for by science fiction and fantasy writers. As a result, Mundane Science Fiction stories usually take place on Earth and in the near future.

But instead of science fiction authors toning down fantasy in order to tell stories of the near future, Design Fiction represents designers amping up speculation to "tell worlds instead of stories," as Bleecker says. Both theories feel a bit scrappy but each highly prizes a type of conceptual rigor: the refusal of Mundane Science Fiction to resort to impossible (and easy) ideas and the dedication of Design Fiction to the meticulous process of making something real.

"Less yammering and more hammering," he likes to say. Both ideas also readily admit to having existed long before they were formally defined, which seems appropriate — naming something as a way of calling it into existence.

And this is a charming aspect of Design Fiction, this act of summoning something into being. By articulating an idea, even an impossible one — by designing and narrativizing it — you make the thing more likely to exist, that particular future more legible. The gap between the present and the near future is ours to traverse at whatever speed we wish, willfully confusing the two, and it is in our hands to evenly distribute William Gibson's future if we so choose. These days it feels as if the future is already here — new products, technologies, and modes of human interaction are constantly being created, often in front of our eyes. Never before has the spectrum between fact and fiction, possible and impossible, realized and unrealized, been more clearly visualized in our daily lives. It is this feeling of imminence — of everything being on the cusp — that Design Fiction revels in. A simple example of this is Kickstarter, where products compete for crowdsourced funding, infiltrating our Facebook feeds with personal entreaties from far-flung acquaintances accompanied by elaborately narrated video pitches. It is a universe of products and ideas that are on the verge of being realized, and are being summoned into existence through storytelling, fundraising, and niche marketing. Another example is the work of Philip Parker — technically the world's most published author — and his algorithmically generated print-on-demand textbooks on every subject imaginable, existing only as Amazon.com listings until one interested person purchases it into existence, often at a ridiculous price. And even online marketplaces like Alibaba.com — a billion dollar enterprise that dwarfs American business-to-business portals — offer products that may or may not exist until enough small businesses have requested a large enough quantity to warrant production. Products exist in a pre-production state, cusping in and out of existence, until the gravitational pull of desire coalesces them into being. These examples may not feel like they represent some spectacular conflation of the present and the future, but they do illustrate how accustomed we have become to dealing in unrealized speculation. In many ways, we have become as comfortable living in the near future as we are living in the present, and this unassuming suspension of disbelief in our daily lives makes even the most fantastic Design Fiction a little easier to accept.

It is a stretch to classify the work of Paul Polak as Design Fiction, but I'd like to reference his treadle pump project as a productive union of design and narrative, to suggest how Design Fiction thinking can easily be applied to situations that are not fantastical or critical, but pragmatic and even banal. As the progenitor of the Design for the Other 90% concept, Polak works on massive design initiatives to end poverty across the world. With IDE, he developed a cost-effective treadle pump that could raise income and productivity throughout developing countries, but for it to be effective for small farmers it had to achieve a certain threshold of name recognition. After trying a number of failed marketing strategies, they hit upon the idea of embedding the product within a Bollywood film to increase awareness. They hired a director, a male and female leads, wrote scripts that displayed the typical full range of life-altering Bollywood drama, commissioned songs written about the treadle pump, choreographed dances, and filmed several fully-realized, fully dramatized films that were shown throughout the Bangladeshi countryside. Millions of people saw these films, played on the back of traveling video-vans, and the movies are credited with the distribution of over two and a half million of the pumps across Asia and Africa.

In this scenario, the relationship between what is fact and what is fiction has been swapped. The treadle pump, a very real object and not fantastical in the least, is treated as the "diegetic prototype," a prop existing in a fictional context in service of a larger narrative. The narrative — a musical about love, loss, and perseverance — is what summons forth the desired future. It may be the most mundane of science fictions, but, as is en vogue these days, not all futures have to be fantastic.

This property swapping, between fictional objects and fictional contexts, is just one example of how Design Fiction aggressively blurs the boundaries between disciplines and calls many discipline-based truths into question. Science fact, for example, is inherently dependent on science fiction, Julian argues. A scientist starts with a hypothesis that is fictional and then works to prove or disprove it, at which point it slides from one end of the science fiction / science fact spectrum to the other. But what happens when you extend the fiction of the experiment further, when you conduct the experiment with wondrously fabricated data, or when you begin with a hypothesis that is seemingly impossible? What happens when science fiction and science fact muddle with each other and swap properties? When a team of scientists, designers, and filmmakers are exploring the future of gestural interfaces in a Hollywood blockbuster, as these technologies are simultaneously being created in the real world — which effort is fueling the other? Or when somewhat debatable science fiction (for example, regarding the relationship between dinosaurs and birds) forever alters the actual scientific debate, and, in fact, the entire world's understanding of an issue — what is the expected responsibility of those who create these fictions?

Julian and his peers at the Near Future Laboratory employ this kind of interdisciplinary thinking in every arena, for various goals including criticism, progress, curiosity, and profit. Some of them conduct workshops with institutions and corporations interested in innovation and speculation. Julian describes his work at Nokia as "ways of enhancing the corporate imagination, swerving conversations to new possibilities that are reasonable but often hidden in the gluttony of overburdened markets of sameness. Running counter to convention is part of what some kinds of science fiction — rather, design fiction — allow for. This is especially valuable in the belly of a large organization with lots of history and lots of convention."

It was in this context that I invited Julian Bleecker into the belly of the Walker Art Center to speak with our staff. Susannah Schouweiler, writer and editor of mnArtists.org, thoughtfully documented his presentation on June 5, 2012, at Walker Art Center, in which he dives into the ideas behind Design Fiction.

Bleecker describes Design Fiction as "the fertile muddle where fact and fiction reflect and influence each other." He says both design and science fiction work to open new lines of conversation, allowing people who are not inclined to think out of the ordinary, to begin to do so. "You can introduce a conversation about something quite speculative; when you're talking about science fiction, no one says, 'that's impossible.' We all understand the normal rules don't apply."

Design Fiction, in particular, he says, "involves thinking of the impossible as not just possible, but *imminent*, even likely." But the work of Design Fiction goes much further than thinking and talking about what might be, building on the ideas that emerge from such speculations: expanding the conversation by making something real, thereby taking it from the gossamer realms of conjecture to the work-a-day spheres of tangible, concrete probability.

"This work involves a symbiotic relationship between design fact and design fiction — things can happen because these conversations are in the world, percolating," he explains. For example, we can see amazing, fictional technology in Hollywood films like *Minority Report*, *2001: A Space Odyssey*, etc. Indeed, that imagined tech is itself a big draw for audiences.

And in a very concrete sense those technologies are real:

Someone designed a product, and designed it with an excruciating level of refinement, not just so it looks good on camera, but in such a way that the whole production team can understand how that tech fits in the story, why it's there … . Using the lexicon established by the film to explain something real, some actual technology, it then becomes legible for a wide audience, because you have a conceptual anchor which introduces that technology (in the case of *Minority Report*, for example, gesture-based interfaces) into the popular imaginary. Bleecker references David A. Kirby, who argues that these elaborately conceived science fiction props — which he calls "diegetic prototypes" — are in a sense superior to the actual working prototypes that scientists and engineers must make to demonstrate the feasibility of a possible technology, for, as Kirby explains "in the diegesis these technologies exist as 'real' objects that function properly and which people actually use."

"The fact that the device you want to make doesn't quite work yet doesn't negate its reality," notes Bleecker, "The conversation, the continuity of relationship between the idea rendered in the film and real technology *is* real … A designer working on that film did enough to get things started to where an industrialist was ready to write a check to develop it for actual use. *That's real.*"

According to Bleecker, Design Fiction involves "extrapolating from known to unknown." Or, as he explains:

> You can introduce a conversation about something quite speculative, but then expand that into an even more fulfilling conversation if you actually *make* the thing you're talking about. It's usually a linear trajectory — from idea to prototype to materialization in some new future. You accrete more meaning in your explanation for what the future might look like as you build, get funding, and create something. You need to get it out of your head; once it's made, you can describe it, *show* it and involve people in a discussion about its specifics.

He muses on the symbiotic interplay between Stanley Kubrick's rigorous scientific speculation in *2001: A Space Odyssey* and the contemporaneous scientific progress of America's space race: "Collapsing science fact together with science fiction to sketch out this trajectory is perhaps the only sensible way to create such a compelling vision whilst on the historical cusp of that vision coming into being."

The Design Fiction process of actually *creating* something — going from conception to execution — facilitates a kind of thoroughness that distinguishes this work from mere speculation. In fact, Bleecker's current interests are anything but remote: he tells us, right now he's most interested in questions about the distribution of innovation. He offers a quote from Gibson by way of explanation: "The future has already arrived, it's just not evenly distributed ... yet."

Bleecker argues that you can disrupt conventional futures with Design Fiction:

> It's fun to look at the world this way, to seek the head-slap moment and play with ideas; but I do think it's also important to consider these things with a code of ethics. You're never just doing it to *do it*, but to make the world a little bit better. Sometimes that's been a very first world thing I've made better because of a new design — like calling your mother gets a little easier, a little better, more enjoyable. But always embedded in the design work is the idea that we're in the business of making things a little more playful, happier, and less unnerving for people. And simply bringing an appreciation of the fact that the future isn't determined, that the future, on an individual scale, is still open to one person's vision of what that can be.

That's valuable in its own right, too. ■

Benjamin H. Bratton
+ Metahaven

META–METAHAVEN
The State *per se*
of Networked Replication

This the third installment in an (unplanned) series of published conversations between myself and designers Metahaven (Daniel van der Velden and Vinca Kruk). The previous two dialogues drew on a shared interest in how cloud computing infrastructures have multiplied and curtailed new kinds of politics, particularly in the nexus between sovereign geographies, network autonomy, and broadband aesthetics. For us, these represent key points on a very short list of most important design issues of our moment. In regard to these, we explored where our intellectual positions and research interests converged and diverged, but without a strong focus on how a specific practice works to explicate and explore these issues. So for this third discussion, the focus is more on Metahaven itself as a design project, and what relation its specific form (as a studio) may have to its specific content (as an intellectual intervention).

BHB

I'd like to take the opportunity to discuss Metahaven, not only specific works, but the project as a whole: *meta-Metahaven*. The story of how the studio started and its path taken through work on Sealand, Wikileaks, and the austerity siege is well covered in other texts, so I would rather focus on where you see the work evolving over time, how it is both timely and untimely.

Is it possible to describe what the Metahaven project is, separate from the collection of works themselves? Is there, or could there ever be, a programmatic thesis as such? (I would only ask that question of a practice such as yours that is so focused and polemic. It would make no sense whatsoever to ask this of 95% of other graphic design studios.)

To answer "no" is, of course, perfectly fine, but It strikes me that there could be a "Metahaven" that isn't doing graphic design, counter-branding and so forth, but is expressed instead through various tools, platforms, networks: Metahaven currency, Metahaven ID, Metahaven apps for Google Glass, etc. all through which the program is consistent. Is this so off base? Is there a scenario in which Metahaven would grow to a population of one hundred, one thousand, or one million?

M

Your question asks if Metahaven could become some sort of sovereign entity, right? Or a fashion label of sorts ... It is tempting and we are thinking about this, but we do so considering where we came from. Our work is about others, not ourselves; that classical graphic design stance is often mistaken for an ethic of modesty, which it isn't; it's a way to remain stealthy.

Metahaven could become a political organization. If anything, it should be that. There is a need for celebrational visual terrorism to deal with today's crazy world. The fact that we mostly work in the English language is at conflict here with the need for such a terrorist organization in the Dutch political context. Ideally we would do it in Dutch, but our thinking is not in Dutch ... sadly.

BHB

One central theme for this exhibition curated by Tim Durfee is design fiction. Design has always relied on rhetorical techniques of the projective, the hypothetical and the futural as essential vocabularies. (It's probably worth another discussion to examine why design's proximity to hypothetical futures, including science fiction, is so topical now and to wonder aloud if this represents a triumph or crisis of imagination.)

But I read the vast majority of your work is straight proposals for things to be implemented immediately. They are not pieces for deferred conversation and negotiation, as in the Dunne & Raby sense of "artifacts from the future". Yours are very sensible observations and techniques for describing and modifying hard reality as it unfolds this very day.

M

We started out as a studio that forward-projected a representative relationship to a potential but very unlikely client. This prospective way of working has a bit of a history in graphic design, but there is no real record of it. Rather than the fictitious, the hypothetical is of interest to us, which could be described as a relationship between potential and reality. Fiction, then, is a form of potential that is linked to reality, in conventional terms at least, by it being a play rather than a real thing. But everyone realizes that it isn't that simple, and fiction can, through some lens and depending on its type, be considered as a potential that could be a reality in certain dicey circumstances. We are most interested in situations where reality approaches fiction and always find such troves of things there which are worth examining, sorting out, or working with, that eventually our practice is indeed not about looking for fiction or for the "What if?" but about the "What now?" Note that that question still leaves plenty of room for the speculative.

BHB

So toward the "What now?" ... The Westphalian model of the State is born in Europe, and it may return to Europe in order to die. One might say that the central figure for Metahaven is not the Internet, *per se*, but the *State*. One could argue that for Metahaven the figure of the Internet is important because of how extends, simulates, displaces, augments, erases, and amplifies the State, perhaps more than the other way around. Would you disagree?

Do you see Metahaven as a project interested in the design and designation of new sovereignties and governmentalities? If so why might that project (or the possibility of that project) be important now, especially, we might say, for a European practice? In what way is it right or wrong to think of Metahaven as a European project in the first place?

M

Metahaven is surely a project of European descent, as it remains obsessed with ruins and ideologies. As a project, it is neither contemporary nor pragmatic. But it is also obsessed with future ruins and fallen goddesses: Rihanna, the Burj Khalifa, Louis Vuitton, and Euroshopper (sadly, that brand has ended). Rather than with states per se, we are perhaps obsessed with the particular form and nature of networks as they pass the threshold of visibility and become almost sovereign: Bitcoin, Silk Road, Mega, the Pirate Bay, WikiLeaks, and how their deeds, words and images are entwined with Karl Marx and Ayn Rand alike. While those groups carve out their temporary sanctuaries in the cloud — gorillavid.in for streaming videos is worth mentioning, as is, of course, PasteBin — there is a permanence to their project that we, altogether, simply love. We love badass network sovereignty. Perhaps it is the kind of sovereignty that nomads have, which is one they don't "legally" have but simply embody by their stance.

BHB

A lot has been said about the Methaven look and feel: the "wrong" aesthetic, the extruded typefaces, the garish gradients, but I want to talk about the form / content problem in a different way. A direct engagement with the meme culture of the web, the hyper-referentiality of the image templates, even the <embed> tag itself, are as important to what you're doing as the semantic content of any one composition: the image of networked image commenting on the networking of the image. The medium of the web is engaged directly as the source, medium and repository of a visual culture, but in ways that are very different from (for example) the New Aesthetic, which emphasizes accidental glitch and machine vision, or the engagement with the noisy pixel as a medium of plastic perception, as for Thomas Ruff's *JPEG* photographs.

M

The New Aesthetic or Post-Internet Aesthetic is a kind of pop art of the Internet, on the Internet, for the Internet. What seems to be missing is the space to reflect and aestheticize the visual forms of commerce that Pop Art appropriated and dragged into the white cube, like Richard Hamilton's *Just What is it That Makes Today's Homes so Different, So Appealing*?

Nevertheless that space to reflect is also the internet. The New Aesthetic, now undead, shows that people have put their memories of the late 90s html aesthetic (combined with the design language of the German "Bauhaus" department store) in the same box as their awareness of the Eurovision Song Contest, M.I.A., Guantanamo Bay, Belarus dictatorships, and Rick Astley. In many ways the New Aesthetic can be seen as the designer punk revenge on Facebook culture — Facebook being ultimately an administrative entity rather than a chosen lifestyle.

At the same time, there are platforms other than the museum and the internet. These are the street, the market, the school, the prison, and such. You might ask what happens to Johnny Cash's work as it moves from the recording studio to the live audience to the prison, and back again. On the Internet and in the gallery, it is a free for all; there hardly is a state change. ∎

STORIED STOREYS
Architecture's Real Fictions

It's hard to believe as you look around. Everything looks so real. Nevertheless, despite this sensation, architecture and the city around you is a form of fiction. It's made up: Imagined first, then constructed.

There are other forms of creative practice that we assume deal with the fictional. Novels, movies, and plays, for example, all (often) take the recognizably real world that we inhabit and tell stories that inhabit this space. In other words, they fictionalize the real. The world is the site within which they manifest their imagination. In order for these fictions to work, they require us to suspend our disbelief. In the process of reading or watching, we are bound to accept their representation of the real world. These forms of art manifest an idea into visible or material form that we can observe from our vantage point as spectators. They rely on armatures and apparatuses such as screen, stage, or gallery to create the sites within which their fictional realities can play out, separated from the "real" world.

But architecture operates in the realm of the real. Unmediated, it is both frame and content simultaneously. We don't have to suspend our disbelief in order for its fiction to be real. In fact, it won't let us believe that it is anything other than entirely real.

Architecture's reality is indistinguishable from the myths that form it. It takes narratives — political, social, economic, cultural — and makes them real. Architecture's power is to transform these abstract concepts into the world. The stories architecture tells are stories that organize us, instruct us, give us identity. They are stories that architecture performs and that it makes us perform.

Its physical fact is so utterly convincing as to obliterate its fictional origin; it seems utterly natural and completely credible. Its power is thus invisible power, naturalizing the myths that precede it into the mundanity of our environment.

Its fictions, though, are rarely spoken of. The absence of discussion of architecture's own fictions serves to preserve its power. Architects' descriptions of space, material qualities, technology, and form as abstract phenomena are ways that they avoid confronting the fact that their work is always essentially a way of writing myth into the world.

But there are traditions within architecture where fiction has been used as a tool to help unlock its inherent power. These are traditions where narrative, scenario, and representation are used to explore the ways in which architecture performs in the world. They also often offer a critical dimension opening a window into architecture's political dimensions.

This can mean architecture as satire, as something closer to science fiction. Here, architectural proposition is intended to provoke, question, and critically discipline. It is intended to change, as well, the perception of our built environments, allowing us to understand them in different ways. Though these projects may never leave the page and remain drawings, they nevertheless can allow us to understand what architecture could be. There has long been a tradition of the drawn speculation in architecture. And often, the powerful ideas contained in these drawings remain significant hundreds of years later. But it was perhaps with Archigram, the British architecture group from 1960s, that the idea of the speculative-critical mode of architectural proposal crystalized. Projects such as David Greene's Log Plug — something disguised as a log that you could plug into for power and data — reads both as a technological proposal and also as a proposition for a networked, nomadic way of life. It explored through architectural speculation the relationship between technology, lifestyle, landscape, and cultural ideas of nature.

Other strands of fiction-oriented architecture explore the architectures' representational qualities. Often, this is an architecture that is hyperconscious of its own performance. It sees itself not only as a building, but also as a representation of a building, simultaneously stage and armature. This is a characteristic of the best Postmodern architecture, which wore it references on its sleeve. This was much more than a series of clever jokes, as Postmodernism is often characterized by those who still find it challenging. I'd argue that this is an architectural version of the Brechtian breach of the fourth wall. It was a moment when architecture turned to its audience and revealed itself in an attempt to express the way cultural fictions shape both architecture itself and the way architecture shapes us.

What has come to be known as design fiction is perhaps a contemporary merging of these two streams. Its project is both technological and cultural and is often concentrated at the intersection of these two ideas.

But let's distinguish between fiction and fantasy here. Fantasy is the point where design fiction tilts into the realm of the self-indulgent. The importance of the fiction is not the fiction itself, but the way that it responds, reacts, and reframes the reality of its circumstance. That is to say, in order to generate critical leverage, architecture's fictions have to operate with specific angles, with sufficient torque, and with particular purchase on their subject. When fiction in architecture, whether sci-fi or historicist, becomes an end in itself, all of the cultural insight and critical power evaporates.

From Archigram through Postmodernism to design fiction, when architecture recasts itself as a fictional enterprise, we suddenly see its technology, space, form, use, and material transformed. They are no longer isolated elements, no longer abstract, but means by which architecture writes its fictions into the world. ■

Fiona
Raby

SYMPOSIUM
KEYNOTE

January 29, 2011

(Excerpt)

I spend much of my time going around, trying to convince designers that fiction is a valuable tool, and I come here and find a whole exhibition celebrating design and fiction. I think it tells us that this space is a space that's opening up for designers to explore much more, which I think is very exciting indeed.

I want to talk about Dunne & Raby's personal position on this because I'm coming from a very 3D background. Tony and I design objects and spaces. We focus closely on products and their context. And I think it's quite a small, narrow area of this much, much bigger area. So when you see the work, it's coming from a very tight focus.

We've been trained in the modernist tradition that says design is about everyday life. That design facilitates the democratization of society. That design is about usefulness. So we get really obsessed with the practicalities of things, even when we're talking about fiction. We ask: Who's it for? What's it for? Do we need it? Who cares? Even when we're talking about this fictional world. We call our little manifesto "fictional functions and functional fictions."

The world of products is obsessed with reality — making things real for people with real needs. And designers can get very upset with the idea that things are not real. But I think it's really difficult to know which bits of reality we actually should be using. So in many ways I think the products at the moment are filled with fictional functions: functions that have no relationship to reality at all. Perhaps they're functions that we desire, but actually they don't play in real life at all. Whereas with functional fictions, these objects are not real. They're prototypes. They don't exist in the world, but perhaps the functions that they address can be very real and very genuine, and I think they can be the kind of useful tools that we use.

Our body of work sits between reality and the impossible. It's a really interesting space to be in. And it's more difficult to navigate in this space than you would imagine. If it's all too fictional, you kind of float about in this space, and you can float off into this fantasy world where no one believes you. But if it's too real, it kind of fits too neatly into the world we know already and, in many ways, we're not being challenged by anything. So it's finding this kind of space.

In many ways, I want to return to these modernist hangups we have about the usefulness of design. Now that we have this space, a space where design can start to play with fiction and reality and we can work out how we use this space, we really must put these narratives to work in some way. And such that they start to have currency and value within much broader contexts outside the context of design. And because we're going to be faced with all these changes and uncertainty, I think that this kind of design has a value within future decision-making processes. And I hope that that's something we can work out how to do. ∎

Benjamin
H. Bratton

PLASTIC FUTURES MARKETS

A droning, monotone voice is recognized by psychiatrists as a symptom of homicidal psychosis. So, too, the entropy haunting contemporary design is a sign of something worse than boredom.

After his junket to #CES2011, Walter Benjamin blogged on the role of utopian futurism in contemporary technoculture: "capitalist design requires a permanent utopia of the object; advertising, product pipelining, speculative prototypes ... today, as all time is capital, so all markets are futures markets."

The syntax of utopia has shifted. The cybernetics of scenario planning has given way to the eschatology of apophenia. Is geopolitics but a dark side of the rainbow effect? With this shift, information becomes unmanageable, nonlinear, associative, arbitrary. Anything is enrolled into the local rhetoric of conspiracy (for meta-addressability, for atemporality, for speculative realist science fiction, for neo-Lysenkoism).

We know that utopias are walled gardens, derived functions of a totality (total boundary, envelope, island, image, law), and suspect that all totalities are at least proto-utopias. This is the crux of Fredric Jameson's field notes on Walmart. This is the alibi of Masdar, New Songdo City, Skolkova, Foxconn. But what do we do with our surplus of utopias? Of totalities multiplied one on top of another into hyperbolic geometries?

Perhaps the real candidate is not the Smart City but Home Depot, and the logistical space of the recombinant object coursing through supply chain heaven. Ponder these warehouse arcades filled with incomplete things with incomplete utility that must be assembled later into metathings in order to be consumed and in order to realize their mission: a factory for 1,023 possible experimental architectures.

Invention depends on the deep recomputability of worldly substance — Catherine Malabou speaks of the world's plasticity. When or where? Less than this, recomputability drives a genuinely new condition to emerge "later in time" at some postponed launch event (next fiscal quarter, after the rebuilding of the temple, the multitude's sovereignty, whatever), it does so "here in space" through the infinite recombinancy of the infinite synchronic field of the longest possible "now." ■

Stuart
Candy[1]

DREAMING TOGETHER

Experiential Futures as a Platform for Public Imagination[2]

In my first year of university, I remember reading *Heart of Darkness* by Joseph Conrad. One passage in particular leapt out at me:

> It is impossible to convey the life sensation of any given epoch of any one's existence — that which makes its truth, its meaning, its subtle and penetrating essence. It is impossible. We live, as we dream — alone.[3]

Something in my 18-year-old mind resonated with this expression of fundamental existential loneliness, which I suspect everyone feels to a degree as they come of age. But these words haunted me for years, and I'm not entirely sure why. It may be that I was grappling with this paradox: Are we truly condemned to live and dream alone? *All of us?* Much more recently, I read a novel by Arthur C. Clarke, *Childhood's End*; a sweeping tale about

humanity being guided to the next phase of its evolution by a mysterious yet seemingly benign alien civilization.[4] The book has stood up well for over 50 years, although of course there's nothing so characteristic of an age's thinking as its science fiction. Clarke is most famous for co-writing with director Stanley Kubrick the epic 1968 film *2001: A Space Odyssey*, and of all sci-fi writers, he strikes me as remarkable for the way his imagination burned to achieve escape velocity from the culture of his era — not to mention his species; to dream a way out into truly different times and places, and take us there.

It was reflecting on Clarke's feats of imagination that got me to wondering about the odd fact that our brains are not temporally bound. There's *no physical limitation* preventing us from cognizing wildly different and yet fully coherent life-settings in detail. Anatomically, human

1   See Contributors, p. 104

2   This paper is based on a presentation at the "Reconstitutional Convention," which inaugurated the Governance Futures Lab at the Institute for the Future in Palo Alto,

California, April 26, 2013. The ideas were further developed through a keynote at the TippingPoint Australia forum "The Future — Unthinkable or Unimaginable" in Canberra, May 29, 2013. Thanks to the organizers of both events.

3   Joseph Conrad, 2007 [1899], *Heart of Darkness*, Penguin Classics, London, p. 33.

4   Arthur C. Clarke, 2010 [1954], *Childhood's End*, Pan Macmillan, London.

brains across the planet, and over tens of thousands of years, haven't really varied much. Yet the variety of worlds — landscapes, cultures, languages, values, technosocial setups — that the human brain has managed to host, to create, and to navigate has been enormous. The very fact that each of us today carries in mind a model of our personal context and surroundings at this historical moment, a world in many ways unimaginable to our ancestors, underlines that in principle we're capable of imagining equally disparate possible worlds of the future — even if we generally don't. It's what our minds are surrounded and scaffolded with that makes all the difference.[5]

"Unimaginable" is not absolute. It's situational. The reason that this matters, I suggest, is that it points to a missing piece in our modern technoculture: I think we have a chronically impoverished practice of public imagination. Yes, there's Arthur C. Clarke, and Godzilla, and *Star Trek*, and many other speculative entertainments before and since; but for "serious" purposes — governance, politics, and the "real" worlds we shape using those processes — we simply have not developed a habit of imagining and sharing the long-range scenarios at issue in any concrete way. Meanwhile, the massive failure to understand our power as a species and to exercise it with anything approaching strategic foresight, let alone wisdom, is producing epically hairy environmental, economic, and other consequences that are increasingly plain to see.

This is not a new line of thought. Noting the curious imbalance that we have countless thousands of history specialists and yet pay scarcely any serious attention to the rest of time, it has now been more than 80 years since the stupendously influential author H.G. Wells (*The War of the Worlds*, *The Time Machine*, *The Invisible Man*) called for Professors of Foresight.[6] Some inroads have been made on that front since; indeed, the entire scholarly field of futures studies, also known as foresight, speaks to the need highlighted by Wells in 1932.[7]

Nigh on half a century has passed since Alvin Toffler observed, in the classic article that led to his 1970 bestseller, *Future Shock*, that

5   It was thanks to years of conversation and collaboration with Dr. Jake Dunagan, now at the Institute for the Future and of California College of the Arts, that this way of thinking about futures as scaffolding for the brain became integral to my own view. See, for example, Jake Dunagan, 2010, "Politics for the Neurocentric Age," *Journal of Futures Studies*, 15(2): 51 – 70, p. 56.

6   "It seems an odd thing to me that though we have thousands and thousands of professors and hundreds of thousands of students of history working upon the records of the past, there is not a single person anywhere who makes a whole-time job of estimating the future consequences of new inventions and new devices. There is not a single Professor of Foresight in the world. But why shouldn't there be? All these new things, these new inventions and new powers, come crowding along; every one is fraught with consequences, and yet it is only after something has hit us hard that we set about dealing with it." H.G. Wells, 1932, 'Wanted — Professors of Foresight!", BBC, 19 November. In: Richard Slaughter (ed.), 1989, *Studying the Future*, Australian Bicentennial Authority / Commission For the Future, Melbourne, pp. 3 – 4.

7   The list of academic foresight programs at the Acceleration Studies Foundation website is a useful resource (though difficult to keep up to date). accelerating. org/gradprograms.html

we have no "heritage of the future."[8] This observation goes right to my point about the need for an overall cultural capacity, toward which an academic field has proven to be only a partial solution: our inherent and permanent lack of a future "heritage" means we have to work hard to create one. And although certainly a challenge, the creation of tangible compensations for our lopsided temporal inheritance can certainly be done, as the emerging practitioners of experiential futures and design fiction are now learning.[9]

It seems to me that the stakes and eventual possibilities for these hybrid forms of design are far greater than one might suspect from watching highly produced videos on the thrilling future of glassware, or prototypes of nifty gestural computer interfaces.[10]

For when it comes to the process of public choice — the way humanity supposedly shapes its destiny in our ostensibly most "developed" communities — we congratulate ourselves on the accomplishment of democracy and fret endlessly over its procedures; the whos and hows of voting; the rituals of deliberation (the weighing of alternatives) and decision (the killing of alternatives when we make a choice).[11] But regardless of who votes, what is the real meaning of any such choices if the alternatives among which we are selecting are underimagined, clichéd — or simply absent?

Whatever their personal shortcomings, I locate the problem not with political candidates but in the scandalously uninspired fodder used to generate public conversation. So where might we look for a solution?

My friend Natalie Jeremijenko, an engineer and artist, has described her work as being about the creation of "structures of participation,"[12] a phrase I use often because to me it captures what good futures

8 "Society has many built-in time spanners that help to link the present generation with the past. Our sense of the past is developed by contact with the older generation, by our knowledge of history, by the accumulated heritage of art, music, literature, and science passed down to us through the years. It is enhanced by immediate contact with the objects that surround us, each of which has a point of origin in the past, each of which provides us with a trace of identification with the past. No such time spanners enhance our sense of the future. We have no objects, no friends, no relatives, no works of art, no music or literature, that originate in the future. We have, as it were, no heritage of the future." Alvin Toffler, 1965, "The future as a way of life." In: Glen Gaviglio and David E. Raye (eds.), 1971, *Society As It Is: A Reader*. Macmillan, New York, pp. 450 – 461, quotation p. 458. [Originally published in *Horizon* 7 (3): 108 – 115.] This same passage appears verbatim in the book: Alvin Toffler, 1970, *Future Shock*. Random House, New York, p. 423.

9 See Stuart Candy, 2010, *The Futures of Everyday Life: Politics and the Design of Experiential Scenarios*. Unpublished doctoral dissertation, Department of Political Science, University of Hawaii at Manoa. scribd.com/doc/68901075/Candy-2010-The-Futures-of-Everyday-Life

10 For a critical view of corporate design fiction, see Noah Raford, 2012, "On Glass & Mud: A Critique of (Bad) Corporate Design Fiction," February 2. news.noahraford.com/?p=1313

11 On the etymology of these terms, see William Isaacs, 1999, *Dialogue: The Art Of Thinking Together*, Doubleday, New York, pp. 37, 45.

12 New York University Steinhardt School of Culture, Education and Human Development website. steinhardt.nyu.edu/faculty_bios/view/Natalie_Jeremijenko

work does, too. Foresight practice involves creating structures of participation for co-imagining. Likewise, the task of governance is bound up with the design and use of structures of participation for collectively shaping the common good. To my mind, those appear in quite diverse forms and at different scales, ranging from the design of a meeting or conference, to the design of a political / legal system like the United States of America, and also to the design of a political and experiential futures intervention like the one I'm about to describe.

With foresight and design colleagues, I have been doing experiential futures since 2006, and its roots and influences go back much further.[13] Of all interventions that I know of in this vein, the most exciting to date is one I heard about shortly after it occurred during the Arab Spring. It is a significant illustration of the faculty of public imagination.[14]

In January 2011, Tunisia ousted President Zine El Abidine Ben Ali, ending a 23-year dictatorship. Immediately, the economy started tanking — the revolutionaries hadn't known they would succeed, and didn't have detailed plans for next steps. With a backdrop of economic suspension and a political vacuum, what followed might have been as bad as what had gone before. What did in fact happen was rather extraordinary.

A month after the revolution, for one day in February 2011, several newspapers and television and radio stations across the country reported as if it were June 16, 2014; three years and four months into the future. They reported stories from within a hypothetical future in which Tunisia enjoyed newfound stability, democracy, and prosperity.

Social media activity swarmed around the #16juin2014 hashtag (and for the first time led the national conversation to trend at number one on French Twitter), and critically, the mood and situation began to change as people imagined and debated the destiny of their country. The intervention also helped spread the call for Tunisians to get back to work, a key step toward recovery in the wake of the upheaval.

This remarkable story should prompt many questions, but the one we're most interested in here is: How might a sustained commitment to structures of participation for public imagination work in other contexts, at scale?

For instance, what if standard political brand-oriented advertising expenditures were curbed, and candidates instead had to produce feature documentaries not about, but from the future that their policies envision?

Most places have a library or museum dedicated to preserving their past; how about a public building dedicated to immersing visitors in an ever-evolving array of experiences of what the community could become one generation from today? Or why couldn't we set aside a public holiday each year, a day dedicated to staging a Festival of Possible Worlds in the streets, parks, and piazzas of great cities around the globe?

Let us return to where we began. It is true that at some level, our personal experience can be only ours. But I no longer fear that we are condemned to dream alone.

13 Candy 2010, op. cit.

14 For more details and sources for this story see Stuart Candy 2012, "An experiential scenario for post-revolution Tunisia," *The Sceptical Futuryst*, April 2. futuryst.blogspot.com/2011/04/experiential-scenario-for-post.html

Candy

DREAMING

I think that humanity is fundamentally *psychedelic* — quite literally: *mind-manifesting*[15] — and that the history we collectively choose to live out in years and decades to come will depend on how well we cultivate public imagination, through experiential futures, large-scale participatory simulations, transmedia games, and the like.

I believe we can dream together, now. And I suspect that to the extent we rise to the challenge of good governance for the 21st century, that's exactly what we will be doing on a regular basis. ■

15 A most elegant statement of this insight comes from the late psychonaut-philosopher Terence McKenna: "[T]echnology is the real skin of our species. Humanity, correctly seen in the context of the last five hundred years, is an extruder of technological material. We take in matter that has a low degree of organization; we put it through mental filters, and we extrude jewelry, gospels, space shuttles. This is what we do. We are like coral animals embedded in a technological reef of extruded psychic objects." Terence McKenna, 1991, *The Archaic Revival*, HarperCollins, New York, p. 93.

Geoff
Manaugh

UNSOLVING THE CITY

An Interview with China Miéville

Novelist China Miéville is widely known, and justifiably celebrated, for his poetic and otherworldly descriptions of urban environments. From floating cities lashed together with ship's hulls to mobile settlements traveling the desert by rail, Miéville's works are filled with architectural and urban imagery that show design fiction at its most exciting and conceptually extreme.

It is all the more interesting to note, however, that one of Miéville's most evocative fictional worlds — the divided city of his 2009 novel, *The City & The City* — attains its conceptual and critical richness precisely by avoiding the standard tropes of a sci-fi metropolis. Rather, disguised as a run-of-the-mill detective story, *The City & The City* pushes an outlandish and Byzantine spatial scenario to the point where speculative political science becomes political science fiction.

In the following interview, excerpted from a discussion originally published on BLDGBLOG, Miéville discusses the narrative potential of spatial critique.

GM

What was your initial attraction to the idea of a divided city?

CM

I first thought of the divided city as a development from an earlier idea I had for a fantasy story. That idea was more to do with different groups of people who live side by side but, because they are different species, relate to the physical environment very, very differently, having different kinds of homes and so on. It was essentially an exaggeration of the

way humans and rats live in London, or something similar. But, quite quickly, that shifted, and I began to think about making it simply human.

For a long time, I couldn't get the narrative. I had the setting reasonably clear in my head and then, once I got that, a lot of things followed. For example, I knew that I didn't want to make it narrowly, allegorically reductive, in any kind of lumpen way. I didn't want to make one city heavy-handedly Eastern and one Western, or one capitalist and one communist, or any kind of nonsense like that. I wanted to make them both feel combined and uneven and real and full-blooded. I spent a long time working on the cities and trying to make them feel plausible and half-remembered, as if they were uneasily not quite familiar rather than radically strange.

I auditioned various narrative shapes for the book and, eventually, after a few months — partly as a present to my Mum, who was a big crime reader, and partly because I was reading a lot of crime at the time and thinking about crime — I started realizing what was very obvious and should have been clear to me much earlier. That's the way that noir and hard-boiled and crime procedurals, in general, are a kind of mythic urbanology, in a way; they relate very directly to cities.

Once I'd thought of that, exaggerating the trope of the trans-jurisdictional police problem — the cops who end up having to be on each other's beats — the rest of the novel just followed immediately. In fact, it was difficult to imagine that I hadn't been able to work it out earlier. That was really the genesis.

GM
One of the most remarkable aspects of the novel is the degree to which you achieve the feel of a fantasy or science fiction story simply through the description of a very convoluted political scenario. The book doesn't rely on monsters, non-humans, magical technologies, and so on; it's basically a work of political science fiction.

CM
This is impossible to talk about without getting into spoiler territory — which is fine, I don't mind that — but we should flag that right now for anyone who hasn't read it and does want to read it.

But, yes, the overtly fantastical element just ebbed and ebbed, becoming more suggestive and uncertain. Although it's written in such a way that there is still ambiguity — and some readers are very insistent on focusing on that ambiguity and insisting on it — at the same time, I think it's a book, like all of my books, for which, on the question of the fantastic, you might want to take a kind of Occam's razor approach. It's a book that has an almost contrary relation to the fantastic, in a certain sense.

GM
In some ways, it's as if *The City & The City* simply describes an exaggerated real-life border condition, similar to how people live in Jerusalem or the West Bank, Cold War Berlin or contemporary Belfast — or even in a small town split by the US / Canada border, like the Stanstead-Derby line. There, the border literally goes through the center of a library. "Technically," the Center for Land Use Interpretation explains, "any time anyone crosses the international line, they are subject to having to report, in person, to a port of entry inspection station for the country they are entering. Visiting someone on the other side of the line, even if the building is next door, means walking around to the inspection station first, or risk being an outlaw." In a sense, these settlements consist of next-door neighbors who otherwise have very complicated spatial and political relationships to one another. For instance, I think I sent you an email about a year ago about a town located both on and between the Dutch-Belgian border, called Baarle-Hertog.

CM
You did!

GM

I'm curious to what extent you were hoping to base your work on these sorts of real-life border conditions.

CM

The most extreme example of this was something I saw in an article in the *Christian Science Monitor*, where a couple of poli-sci guys from the State Department or something similar were proposing a solution to the Arab-Israeli conflict. In the case of Jerusalem, they were proposing basically exactly this kind of system, from *The City & The City*, in that you would have a single urban space in which different citizens are covered by completely different juridical relations and social relations, and in which you would have two overlapping authorities.

I was amazed when I saw this. I think, in a real-world sense, it's completely demented. I don't think it would work at all, and I don't think Israel has the slightest intention of trying it.

My intent with *The City & The City* was, as you say, to derive something hyperbolic and fictional through an exaggeration of the logic of borders, rather than to invent my own magical logic of how borders could be. It was an extrapolation of really quite everyday, quite quotidian, juridical and social aspects of nation-state borders: I combined that with a politicized social filtering and extrapolated out and exaggerated further on a sociologically plausible basis, eventually taking it to a ridiculous extreme.

But I'm always slightly nervous when people make analogies to things like Palestine because I think there can be a danger of a kind of sympathetic magic: you see two things that are about divided cities, and so you think that they must therefore be similar in some way.

Whereas, in fact, in a lot of these situations, it seems to me that — and certainly in the question of Palestine — the problem is not one population being unseen, it's one population being very, very aggressively seen by the armed wing of another population.

In fact, I put those words into Borlu's mouth in the book, where he says, "This is nothing like Berlin, this is nothing like Jerusalem." That's partly just to disavow — because you don't want to make the book too easy — but it's also to make a serious point, which is that, obviously, the analogies will occur but sometimes they will obscure as much as they illuminate.

GM

Your books often lend themselves to political readings, on the other hand. Do you write with specific social or political allegories in mind, and, further, how do your settings — as in *The City & The City* — come to reflect political intentions, spatially?

CM

My short answer is that I dislike thinking in terms of allegory, quite a lot. I've disagreed with Tolkien about many things over the years, but one of the things I agree with him about is this lovely quote where he talks about having a "cordial dislike for allegory."

The reason for that is partly something that Fredric Jameson has written about, which is the notion of having a master code that you can apply to a text and which, in some way, solves that text. At least in my mind, allegory implies a specifically correct reading, a kind of one-to-one reduction of the text.

It amazes me the extent to which this is still a model by which these things are talked about, particularly when it comes to poetry. This is not an original formulation, I know, but one still hears people talking about "what does the text mean?" — and I don't think text means like that. Texts do things.

I'm always much happier talking in terms of metaphor, because it seems that metaphor is intrinsically more unstable. A metaphor fractures and kicks off more metaphors, which kick off more metaphors, and so on. In any fiction or art at all, but particularly in fantastic or imaginative work, there will inevitably be ramifications, amplifications, resonances, ideas, and riffs that throw out these other ideas. These may well be deliberate; you may well be deliberately trying to think about issues of crime and punishment, for example, or borders, or memory, or whatever it might be. Sometimes, they won't be deliberate. But the point is, those riffs don't reduce. There can be perfectly legitimate political readings and perfectly legitimate metaphoric resonances, but that doesn't end the thing. That doesn't foreclose it. The text is not in control. Certainly the writer is not in control of what the text can do — but neither, really, is the text itself.

So I'm very unhappy about the idea of allegoric reading, on the whole. Certainly I never intend my own stuff to be allegorical. Allegories, to me, are interesting more to the extent that they fail, to the extent that they spill out of their own bounds. Reading someone like George MacDonald — his books are extraordinary — or Charles Williams. But they're extraordinary to the extent that they fail or exceed their own intended bounds as Christian allegory.

When Iron Council came out, people would say to me: "Is this book about the Gulf War? Is this book about the Iraq War? You're making a point about the Iraq War,

aren't you?" And I was always very surprised. I was like, listen: if I want to make a point about the Iraq War, I'll just say what I think about the Iraq War. I know this because I've done it. I write political articles. I've written a political book. But insisting on that does not mean for a second that I'm saying — in some kind of unconvincing, "cor-blimey, I'm just a storyteller, guvnor" type thing — that these books don't riff off reality and don't have things to say about it.

There's this very strange notion that a writer needs to smuggle these other ideas into the text, but I simply don't understand why anyone would think that that's what fiction is for. So, when people say, "Are you really talking about this?" my answer is generally not no, it's generally "yes, but," or "yes, and," or "yes ... but not in the way that you mean."

GM

Let's go back to the idea of the police procedural. It's intriguing to compare how a police officer and a novelist might look at the city — the sorts of details they both might notice or the narratives they both might pick up on. Broadly speaking, each engages in detection — a kind of hermeneutics of urban space. How did this idea of urban investigation — the "mythic urbanology" you mentioned earlier — shape your writing of The City & The City?

CM

On the question of the police procedural and detection, for me, the big touchstones here were detective fiction, not real police. Obviously they are related, but they're related in a very convoluted, mediated way.

What I wanted to do was write something that had a great deal of fidelity — hopefully not camp fidelity, but absolute, rigorous fidelity — to certain generic protocols of policing and criminology. That was the drive, much more than trying to find out how police really do their investigations. The way a cop inhabits the city is doubtless a fascinating thing, but what was much more important to me for this book was the way that the genre of crime, as an aesthetic field, relates to the city.

The whole notion of decoding the city — the notion that, in a crime drama, the city is a text of clues, in a kind of constant quantum oscillation between possibilities, with the moment of the solution really being a collapse and, in a sense, a kind of tragedy — was really important to me.

Of course, I'm not one of those writers who says I don't read reviews. I do read reviews. I know that some readers were very dissatisfied with the strict crime drama aspect of it. I can only hold up my hands. It was extremely strict. I don't mean to do that kind of waffley, unconvincing, writerly, carte blanche, get-out-clause of "that was the whole point." Because you can have something very particular in mind and still fuck it up.

But for me, given the nature of the setting, it was very important to play it absolutely straight so that, having conceived of this interweaving of the cities, the actual narrative itself would remain interesting, and page-turning, and so on and so forth. I wanted it to be a genuine who-dunnit. I wanted it to be a book that a crime reader could read and not have a sense that I had cheated.

By the way, I love that formulation of crime-readers: the idea that a book can cheat is just extraordinary.

GM
Can you explain what you mean, in this context, by being rigorous? You were rigorous specifically to what?

CM
The book walks through three different kinds of crime drama. In section one and section two, it goes from the world-weary boss with a young, chippy sidekick to the mismatched partners who end up with grudging respect for each other. Then, in part three, it's a political conspiracy thriller. I quite consciously tried to inhabit these different iterations of crime writing, as a way to explore the city.

But this has all just been a long-winded way of saying that I would not pretend or presume any kind of real policing knowledge of the way cities work. I suspect, probably, like most things, actual genuine policing is considerably less interesting than it is in its fictionalized version — but I honestly don't know.

GM
There's a book that came out a few years ago called *The Meadowlands*, by Robert Sullivan. At one point, Sullivan tags along with a retired detective in New Jersey who reveals that, now that he's retired, he no longer really knows what to do with all the information he's accumulated about the city over the years. Being retired means he basically knows thousands of things about the region that no longer have any real use for him. He thus comes across as a very melancholy figure, almost as if all of it was supposed to lead up to some sort of narrative epiphany — where he would finally and absolutely understand the city — but then retirement came along and everything went back to being slightly pointless. It was an interpretive comedown, you might say.

CM
That kind of specialized knowledge, in any field, can be intoxicating. If you experience a space — say,

a museum — with a plumber, you may well come out with a different sense of the strengths and weaknesses of that museum — considering the pipework, as well, of course, as the exhibits — than otherwise. This is one reason I love browsing specialist magazines in fields about which I know nothing.

Obviously, then, with something that is explicitly concerned with uncovering and solving, it makes perfect sense that seeing the city through the eyes of a police detective would give you a very self-conscious view of what's happening out there.

In terms of fiction, though, I think, if anything, the drive is probably the opposite. Novelists have an endless drive to aestheticize and to complicate. I know there's a very strong tradition — a tradition in which I write, myself — about the decoding of the city. Thomas de Quincey, Michael Moorcock, Alan Moore, Neil Gaiman, Iain Sinclair — that type of thing. The idea that, if you draw the right lines across the city, you'll find its Kabbalistic heart, and so on.

The thing about that is that it's intoxicating — but it's also bullshit. It's bullshit and it's paranoia — and it's paranoia in a kind of literal sense, in that it's a totalizing project. As long as you're constantly aware of that, at an aesthetic level, then it's not necessarily a problem; you're part of a process of urban mythologization, just like James Joyce was, I suppose. But the sense that this notion of uncovering — of taking a scalpel to the city and uncovering the dark truth — is actually real, or that it actually solves anything, and is anything other than an aesthetic sleight of hand, can be quite misleading, and possibly even worse than that. To the extent that those texts do solve anything, they only solve mysteries that they created in the first place, which they scrawled over the map of a mucky contingent mess of history called "the city". They scrawled a big question mark over it, and then they solved it.

Arthur Machen does this as well. All the great weird fiction city writers do it. Machen explicitly talks about the strength of London, as opposed to Paris, in that London is more chaotic. Although he doesn't put it in these words, I think what partly draws him to London is this notion that, in the absence of a kind of unifying vision, like Haussmann's boulevards, and in a city that's become much more syncretic and messy over time, you have more room to insert your own aestheticizing vision.

As I say, it's not in and of itself a sin, but to think of this as a real thing — that it's a lived political reality or a new historical understanding of the city — is, I think, a misprision. ∎

Geoff
Manaugh

EXPANSIONARY TALES

3D-printing bees, their stomachs heavy with genetically modified concrete, build whole new urban neighborhoods on the shores of Tokyo Bay. Trap-streets flash into being for one night — and one night only — before refolding themselves back into the autumn cracks of north London. Neutrino storms thunder and torque through artificial caves carved beneath Manhattan by the Department of Energy. Bioluminescent kudzu overruns the brick walls of Philadelphia, escaped from an amateur seed lab; children tend glowing forests in the frames of abandoned buildings.

The use of speculative non-fiction and documentary myths to catalyze new possibilities for design is increasingly central to the spatial and industrial arts. More than critique, more than nostalgia, more even than technical expertise, what we need now is a liberatory set of expansionary tales — random briefs, diagnostic provocations, surrogate purposes, and augmented constraints — pushing once again at the conceptual frontiers of architecture, literature, film, engineering, art, biology, physics, and design.

Stolen periscopes, installed upside-down on the sidewalks of Istanbul, show pedestrians the city's cellars, crypts, subways, and buried streams; they are soon more popular than TV. GPS-stabilized bridges of human bone construct themselves across the Pacific, webbing San Francisco to Sydney. Drone submarines filled with intelligent, neuro-chemical mists pass unseen through the Arctic Sea.

Fictions are the truths we tell ourselves in order to reveal the next steps to take — hurling counterfeit handholds forward into a world that, in turn, demands its own emerging sets of extrapolations and speculations. ∎

Peter
Lunenfeld

BESPOKE FUTURES

■ Adapted from *Bespoke Futures: Media Design and the Vision Deficit*, 2007.

UP

MADE

Over the last quarter-century, far-sighted multinationals have used scenario planning to ponder upcoming conditions and their effects on long-term profit and loss. Some of the better-known successes of the process were Royal Dutch Shell's planning for global oil demands after the price shocks of the 1970s, scenario planning by the South African government under apartheid that enabled them to contemplate a peaceful turnover of power to Nelson Mandela and the African National Congress, and the development of Smith & Hawkins in the 1990s, based on analyses of the growing market for aging, property-owning baby-boomers.

I'm interested in subverting the methodologies of corporate scenario planning to create what I call bespoke futures — scenarios that go beyond profit and loss to create an opportunity space for the imagination. To do so, I détourne Peter Schwartz's book *The Art of the Long View: Planning for the Future in an Uncertain World*, which distills the decades-long work of his consultancy, the Global Business Network (GBN). ■

~~Stay Focused~~
Stay Visionary

~~Keep It Simple~~
Keep It Complex

~~Keep It Interactive~~
Design It Interactive

~~Plan to Plan and Allow Enough Time~~
Plan for Serendipity and Allow
    Enough Space

~~Don't Settle for a Simple High,
    Medium, and Low Plots~~
Aim High

~~Avoid Probabilities or "Most Likely"
    Plots (Key advice: "Don't fixate
    on just one scenario that you
    want to achieve.")~~
Fixate on Just One Scenario that
    You Want to Achieve

~~Avoid Drafting Too Many Scenarios~~
Draft Enough Scenarios to Kill All
    But the Best

~~Invent Catchy Names for the
    Scenarios~~
Invent Catchy Visuals for the
    Scenarios

~~Make the Decision Makers Own the
    Scenarios~~
Own Your Own Scenarios

~~Budget Sufficient Resources for
    Communicating the Scenarios~~
Generate Sufficient Fervor to
    Communicate the Scenarios

GUISES OF THE CASTLE

"Death, masks, makeup, all are parts of the festival that subverts the order of the city."[1] We would like to add "guises" to this Derridian list. Guises are subversive but do not cause chaos where there is system or generate fake where there is real. Guises are not subversive in that they oppose what is called essence or identity; rather, they question the concept of essence, of stable identity. Especially since the breakthrough of modernity, identity has turned out to be a difficult figure to fix. First there was mistrust in traditional metaphysical systems; then came the discovery of the unconscious, and later the determination through language; and, finally, the media universe. All of these breaks imply that identity is but a dynamic series of various guises. And there is no object behind these guises, but only semblances in relation to other ones.

In this sense, we don't want to talk "meta" about guises. We don't want to theorize guises, because that would actually mean to search for their essence. Rather, we propose to introduce a concrete relation of guises within Franz Kafka's novel fragment The Castle[2] and the objects we developed in response.

The Castle is no castle as we imagine it, but rather an unrepresentative, old, and shabby structure. It consists of numerous single buildings with remarkably many corridors and small rooms. To the foreigner K., the tower looks like a usually hidden roommate that is escaping through the roof.

To gain access to the Castle, K. decides to stay in a snowy village nearby, although he is not very welcome. The village is obviously structured by complex rules of a national state, and in the hostel he asks for a residence permit that he does not hold. As small as the village appears, so immense must be the bureaucratic apparatus behind it. After an obscure telephone conversation with the Castle administration, K. is sent two assistants. Yet it is not clear if he is allowed to stay. Throughout the novel, K.'s identity remains vague; he claims to be a land surveyor, yet he has no instruments. He does not do any

1   Jacques Derrida, Barbara Johnson: Dissemination, New York: Continuum International Publishing Group, 2004, p.142

2   Franz Kafka: Das Schloß. Roman in der Fassung der Handschrift, S. Fischer, 1982 Das Schloß was written in 1922 and first published in a shortened version in 1926, posthumously by Max Brod. Only in 1982, S. Fischer Verlag published a version of Kafka's original manuscript.

work, but he receives a letter from the Castle saying that they are pleased with his service. He takes a temporary job as the school attendant, only to be fired right away. K. starts an affair with the waitress Frieda, although she is the lover of an important administrative authority from the Castle — a fact that could undermine all of his efforts. This, however, is also not the essence of the story. Again, the Castle is just a play of guises in which K. does not find any orientation. He arguably breaks the rules, and he insults the village people. Yet all of this does not matter. The only thing we can observe is this paradoxical figure. The more K. tries to achieve his goal, the more he distances himself from it. Communication is without any result: the real is full of the surreal. If there is established a certain relation in one scene, it is dissolved in the next one. There are details that K. understands, yet the whole structure remains obscure and even absurd to him.

The Castle is a totality of guises, a series of references heard, seen, felt, and lived in the village. The Castle is omnipresent without being there; it is omniscient and still commits errors. It is omnipotent, although its staff is overtired and oversensitive. The Castle is an interior that also includes the village. At one point we read that the village is the Castle's property, who lives or stays here, virtually lives or stays in the Castle. Then again, the Castle appears as a pretty miserable small town, cobbled together out of village houses, distinguished only in that everything is built of stone.

The Castle is also an outside. K. entered the Castle when he crossed the bridge to take the path that leads to the Castle. Yet he arrives at the village without actually accessing its community. It is an outside in the guise of various interiors that K. is confronted with. It is private spaces that are structured as an institution. At the same time, it is a bureaucratic monster that inhabits a village. The Castle is invisible, although its structure is materialized in every object, architecture, and habitude. The village people live their lives under the virtual shadow of the Castle's authority, although this power is never executed. The Castle is a myth even as it is composed of the most banal and everyday life, which takes place in hostels, schools, and private houses. It is an authoritarian system of order although the rules remain abstract, nebulous, and even out of control. The hostess admits that there might be the possibility to get somewhere with a breach of the rules and the traditions, but she has never experienced something like that — although there might be examples, maybe.

From the beginning, K. aims at interpreting the paradoxical guises of the Castle in order to reveal its essence. He does not recognize that he doesn't change his initial image of it. The contrary holds true: he regards his preconceived opinion as confirmed. In the end, the Castle reveals itself to be nothing but different guises of K.'s search for his own identity. But of this search, nothing remains.

K. fails. If we take him as a typically modern figure, we are back to where we started: Derrida describes modernity's own failure with its persistent belief that reality is singular — just like K. assumes the Castle to be one reality, open to access. It is his obsession with this goal that actually makes K. fail, because it makes him ignore that his reality is about individual, different, and even paradoxical guises within the village. His failure is our lesson for today. K. fails, as modernity fails for Derrida, because of an ego that stands in the way of attention — attention for the heterogeneous, the fragmentary, the marginal, the absurd. ■

Norman M. Klein

DEAD RECKONING

The Endless
Rediscovery of America

How do we isolate narrative structures where fact and fiction utterly coexist? It is not as simple a prospect as one might assume. I do not propose that we return to the heritage of post-structuralism, to a discourse about simulacra or floating signifiers. Theories of globalism are more appropriate, particularly when we consider financial derivatives as a place where fictions were facts that crashed the world economy.

But there is a problem in simply naming the process in terms of late twentieth-century century globalism. In many respects that still presumed, as its epic story, that the Enlightenment tradition of epistemology was slipping. We are past that in-between moment now; the Enlightenment tradition has surely ended. To retain strict rules, even an ethic, inside that tradition, the narrative distance between fiction and scientific were kept profoundly separate; that was essential to Enlightenment method, even to its poetics, its literature. But over the past 40 years, under the dissolving effect of media, communications technology, and new modes of economic power, that distinction, as a basis for dialectic study, seems to be lost.

59

We have a problem even giving names to the new poetics where fact and fiction coexist — the narrative grammar of this new civilization. I have used terms like "scripted spaces," "the social imaginary," "emerging urban-industrial feudalism." There are another fifty terms to be found in media studies, in biopolitics (as a field), in ludic theories of collective play, in dozens of books about gaming and games. For this anthology, editor Tim Durfee posited the term "made-up," to isolate how design is caught up in this ficto-factual mix. That reminds me of "legal fiction," an untruth that is even more legally solid than a fact; like a financial derivative, for example. Apparently, the term *fictio* existed in ancient Roman law, to isolate such cases: a jurisprudence of case law where fictions defined one's legal rights.

So let us, for the moment, substitute the term "made-up" with "legal fiction." For the sake of brevity, we concoct a "true" history of legal fictions; then narrow to a case study about the Americas. In order to tell our story honestly, we try out a mode of writing that is both fictional and historically factual, researched carefully, where it is difficult for the reader to identify which is which, like a card trick up close.

The most suitable opening for this history — the legal fiction that I wish were true — was told to me in 2008 by a Portuguese diplomat stationed in London. He said that on February 18, 1493, an unknown ship tried to anchor near the island of Santa Maria in the Azores. In accordance with laws of the sea, the captain sent a polite message to shore, as a maritime civility. In the message, he said that his vessel (which was a Spanish three-masted caravel, quite typical in that part of the world) had been damaged by a great storm and needed provisions.

But the people of the Azores didn't believe a word of it. They had been warned by the king of Portugal to trust no one. These islands were vulnerable, hundreds of miles from nowhere. Maps had been citing them for almost a thousand years, but essentially no one tried to live there until 1430. That is, only 60 years before 1493 had these islands actually been settled by human beings. The Azores were, in fact,

60

the very last piece of Europe to be "discovered." But why so long: why, many asked, had it had taken a thousand years to occupy them? The Irish had been there in 550. According to Irish legend, the islands had once been attached to the continent. But as of 1493, they were not even attached to the ocean floor; the islands were like algae, literally floating away from Europe.

The soil was also rocky, often subject to landslides and severe wind. That made harvests oppressive. Luckily, over the previous two years, the yield for olives, and the population of sheep, had improved somewhat. But Azoreans were mountain settlers struggling on a volcanic edge of the world. They believed, as a matter of faith, that nothing good can last. Therefore, without a doubt, this ship was a bad omen. It was obviously a pirate vessel. There was no other logical explanation. Why does a captain intentionally steer very far to the west, directly into ocean storms, except to hide his presence, like a thief?

The captain, meanwhile, was grateful to have a ship still floating at all. He sent a few of his men to the island of Santa Maria to offer thanks to the Holy Virgin. But the men were immediately arrested and imprisoned. The governor of the island then ordered the captain to surrender for trial. However, the captain was famously a stubborn man. He would not budge. He even refused to allow any Portuguese to board. Obviously (logic suggested), he was hiding something quite valuable — or unholy.

At this point of the narrative, I find conflicting stories: In most versions, the captain gives his name as Colón, or even Zarpa. Then there is a blank that has persisted for over 500 years. Official records were faked or lost. Historians cannot be certain. The arguments are still raging.

This man, Colón, was obviously Christopher Columbus, an admiral working for the crown of Spain. Somehow, Colón had married a Portuguese woman in 1479, a very well-born member of the Portuguese court. Yet Colón himself was very lowly, the son of a weaver from Genoa, and practically illiterate. Nevertheless, his logs reveal a man who could write Spanish elegantly.

61

That is the standard version of Columbus: a seat-of-the-pants genius. He could sail by dead reckoning. Even when he missed the mark, he found something better instead. On the way to Asia, without maps or the stars to guide him, he accidentally bumped into islands off the coast of North America. On the way home, through disabling storms, he bumped into the Azores, an island chain 900 miles from Lisbon.

This Columbus was presumably a kind of idiot savant. He is said to have died convinced that Cuba was part of Asia. By 1520, it was Vespucci's name, not Columbus' name, that came to represent the New World.

Then there are the hundred other versions: Columbus as a Jewish converso; or as a Muslim sympathizer; or a Spaniard, not an Italian. And most recently, in a controversial (and carefully researched) book entitled *The Columbus Mystery Revealed*, he is the Portuguese son of the king of Poland, who was actually Lithuanian. The author, Manuel da Silva Rosa, has stirred diplomatic tension between Portugal, Italy, and Spain and was honored in Lithuania. To which of these nations does the official identity of Columbus belong? This is not a small matter. Columbus is the blue-chip indicator for every imagined America.

Columbus is the ultimate legalized fiction, arguably the most subjunctive figure in world history. In 1792, in Boston, at the third centenary of his first voyage, Columbus was essentially canonized by the Episcopalian elite. Thereafter, the myth of Columbus is joined to the new republic. His undaunted generosity presumably launched the civilizing mission that led to democracy in the United States.

At the same time, James Fenimore Cooper writes in 1838 that all literature about Columbus — from history to fiction — inspires "a disposition to deny": "After carefully perusing several of the Spanish writers — from Cervantes to the translator of Columbus, the Alpha and Omega of peninsula literature," and after having read premier histories by Americans "from beginning to end, we do not find a syllable ... that we understand to be conclusive evidence."

That incorrigible absence of finality tells a different kind of tale, which brings us back to the matter of legalized fiction — and I do mean final, as if the fiction were settled in a court of law. Literary historian Roberto González Echevarría offers a thread in his splendid *Myth and Archive: A Theory of Latin American Narrative* (1980) that helps clarify the issue. Among many sources, he refers to a novel just published in 1980 — *El arpa y la sombra*, by Cuban Magic Realist Alejo Carpentier — about Pope Pius IX being unable to decide if he should take steps toward recognizing (canonizing) Columbus as a saint. Echevarría sees this conceit as the summation of a peculiar twist in Latin American law; or rather, law as fiction. During the Spanish occupation, over 300 years, official reports were sent out to the king of Spain from Mexico that were littered with fictions. It was terra cognita: the unfindable map of the unknowable world given official sanction. These reports then circulated throughout the Spanish Americas to help convert the native people in tiny villages, to bring peace to the faithful.

Indeed, the fictive kingdoms of Latin America were archived officially as fact; this was standard practice. And finally, by 1700, the tone of these untrue legal facts was incorporated into Latin American picaresque fiction. The official reporters, known as *relaciónes*, became essentially the narrators of fanciful tales.

The examples that follow, across an ocean of sources from literature to cultural history, would overwhelm this brief essay. Let me summarize in this way: All cultures rely on legal fictions to some degree. It is an old fiction writer's trick to justify the impossible by finding a quote in the newspaper, particularly from a newspaper of record. One finds that often in fantasy realism from Nikolai Gogol, because in Russia during the 1830s (as in Soviet newspapers a century later), all official reports were a game, even a ludic pleasure, to second-guess what was left out or bluntly replaced.

We turn to our beleaguered fourth estate today, our depleted news-gathering sources, and to the oatmeal of Internet factoids that snow blind us every 24 hours — the famous 24-hour news cycle, the land of legalized fiction. During those 24 hours, any non-truth is allowable, especially when the subject is politics, sovereignty, money, labor,

63

scandal. But if it is a murder, objectivity prevails. One has to withhold judgment for a day or two. However, news media will cheerfully carry water for political pundits and liars of inconsolable mediocrity.

You ask viewers what they think. Everyone seems to take the news with a grain of salt. What does this grumpy obedience mean? We accept almost nihilistically, like Azoreans in my imaginary 1493, that there is no longer a true measure of events. We may get an official retraction tomorrow, but it will arrive too late. It is now established that Obamacare will double the cost of student loans, and so on. All facts increasingly resemble a first draft that never can be revised. It is like telling the jury (in the ultimate version of legalized fiction) to disregard the evidence just presented.

As authors, designers, filmmakers, and scholars, how should we gauge the history of legalized fiction, of the made-up story? It is certainly good material — enough misery and perverse adventure for any writer of fiction. What a price we pay. We are no longer citizens; we are audience. Apparently, the agency of the Internet doesn't help the general public arrive at the truth in time, because truth is not the point. Citizens of the United States, as heir to the legalized fiction that is America, love the charm of the official lie, the performance of untruth. They always did. Edgar Allan Poe loved a hoax, especially when it originated in the newspaper.

Legalized fiction, when it turns into entertainment spectacle, is tough, surgical, pretentious, populist. It is like TV characters we trust because they are so unreliable. They are like us. They don't need a third act; the same first act is always enough. However, the cost of legalized fictions, in dollars and moral capital, is immeasurable — until the bills arrive.

By the way, Manuel Rosa, the author of the new Columbus history, the Columbus who is a Portuguese nobleman, son of Lithuanian king of Poland, was himself born in the Azores. Clearly, the Internet is now a floating kingdom like the Azores. The reader might be wondering how I got hold of that fact from the collective memory of Azoreans in 1493. But to leave such facts suspended in that way — with spaces between — is part of how the archive of history is constructed. Historians are constantly facing these gaps: a truly vital piece of evidence was destroyed, or not taken seriously ... at first. And today, in 2013, media designers are inheriting that archival irony. Let me summarize by positing that in databases and social networks, legal fictions as archive grow ever more ponderous — or should I say treacherous? The scale of made-up legal fiction has finally encircled our planet, very much like a carbon footprint.

We return, with a feather's touch, to 1200 this time. Once again, ships escape beneath the horizon. Clearly, the world is curved at least. People knew that for millennia. However, Europeans, even Venetians who traveled a lot, did not know of enough earth to fill the curve. There was a lost world, or worlds, hiding from us.

For centuries, theories abounded on how to capture that lost curve of the earth. World mapping was very much a fiction. There is no doubt that terra incognita maps of all kinds, mental and physical, were in abundance by 1492 — often called *mappa mundi*. Indeed, the legal fiction that would become the Americas was already there to see, at least 300 years before Columbus set sail for the Indies. How we love those lost worlds, where Vikings and Chinese and Irish sailors disappear into immeasurable space.

In 1882, Ignatius Donnelly (schemer, promoter, writer, politician) found Atlantis. He described a giant kingdom underwater, over 2,000 miles long, the ultimate lost world. Its eastern boundary was the Azores; the western boundary was Long Island. It is rumored that ocean liners used to announce where they were, relative to Atlantis, and then make soundings into the lost, antediluvian kingdom on the ocean floor.

Similarly, Columbus may have thought that he was sailing into a new Crusade, to find a way to Jerusalem through a back door. It would be a surprise attack, a bypass of the Ottoman control of the eastern Mediterranean. More accurately, though, it was Columbus' reenactment of a standard feature within these *mappa mundi*, these maps of the unfindable curve of the earth. At the center, very often, was Jerusalem, where all biblical fiction was legally a fact.

65

Jerusalem and Rome and China are indeed the rivals of this imaginary America, this "pristine" wilderness, as it was called in nineteenth-century America — meaning uncivilized, waiting for redemption by white, European democracy. And all of them were fully integrated into the legal fictions surrounding Columbus; they were the background to the discovery of America.

Now we face another haunting: the remains of the fact-driven civilization identified with the eighteenth century forward; the ruin of a modernist world once dominated by print and electoral democracy (and imperialism, etc.). Our passage through this emerging feudal world is already eerie more than ebullient. As a final statement, in passing, allow me to conclude in this way: Let us suppose that the imaginary America (1200 – 2050) were to actually disappear — and by that I mean not the United States vanishing, but rather the legal fiction of America, the myths of freedom and discovery that led to its settlement. All the perversity and yearning ends. Afterward, with a collective premonition like bees in a hive, our species would have to replace the imaginary America. The alternative, of course, would have to discover two lost continents and invent from there.

Now that would be a challenge, a legal and moral fiction worth trying out.

■

07–11–13   67

EXCERPTS

From the
MOS
Office Policy

MOS
Office Policy
Expurgated Version

68   MOS

Dear Employee or Other Interested Party,

Policies are put in place to serve you, the employee (hereafter called "you"), and our firm. (See Appendix 11.0 "How to Read the Policy.") MOS (hereafter called "the Office") is a growing and changing architectural firm that wishes to construct a progressive, architectural avant-garde. This avant-garde has its own desires to exist after, and in a funny way because of, the previous "opportunistic" practice generation of architects and the exhaustion of the digital Rococo. (See Appendix 5.1 "Seven Habits of Highly Annoying Digital Rococo People" (HADRP), Appendix 2.8 "How to Talk to Members of the Practice Generation" (PG), and Flowchart 1.3 "Nineties vs. Noughties.") While we cannot have an Office Policy (hereafter called "the Policy") that covers every possibility, eventuality, or human need, we do have leadership (hereafter called "the Principals") that will listen and endeavor to make appropriate decisions that are fair to you and the Office. Therefore, this Policy is not a contract, and it is not binding. It is merely a set of guidelines that may be altered at any time, without notice. More than anything, the Policy expresses the right and obligation of the Principals to interpret and modify the Policy when individual needs or the Office's well-being are at stake — which, to be honest, happens all the time.

You should subscribe to the following guidelines that constitute the Policy:

PART 1
Employment Status,
Hiring Criteria, Termination

1   The Office adheres to all local, state and federal laws including the Civil Rights Act of 1964, the Age Discrimination in Employment Act of 1967 (ADEA), the Rehabilitation Act of 1973, the Americans with Disabilities Act (ADA) of 1990, and the ADA Amendments Act of 2008. These acts could also be said to inform a more general inclusivity that extends to the formal and organizational techniques we employ in our work. (See §§ 1– 3 and Appendix 3.7 "The Exclusion of Inclusionary Models.")

2   The Office strongly supports all disciplinary minorities. We are for the rough over the smooth, the polychromatic over the glossy white, and the primitive and awkward over the sophisticated and elegant. (See Appendix 7.2 "No Composing

70   MOS

Colors Pictorially — Monochromatic is Polychromatic is, etc.")

3   Termination can result from, but is not lim-ited to, documented and undocumented cases of the following:

☐ Poor Performance (PP)
☐ Lack of Accountability and Thought (LACT)
☐ Unexcused Creative Absenteeism (UCAB)
☐ Illegal Acts (ILLACTs)
☐ Falsification of Facts (FOFs)
☐ Unauthorized Destruction of Office Property (UDOP)
☐ Demise of the Architectural Profession (DAP)
☐ Excessively Professional Behavior (EPB)
☐ Improper Use or Distribution of the Office Policy (IUDOP)
☐ Egregious Taste in Music (ETM)
☐ Circumstances Beyond Our Control (CBOC)

PART 3
Approaches to Production,
Addiction, Elimination and Recycling

1   The Office supports and is supported by narratives — in particular, narratives that go nowhere. You should know that the production of fictitious, misread,

referential storylines from history, contemporary events, art criticism and sci-fi is
an important component of our work. (See
Appendix 12.3 "Lost Cats and Women
Who Disappear Suddenly in the Work of
Haruki Murakami.") Understanding that
the gathering of new material is crucial
to the success of the firm, you may be
required to attend obscure and unpopular
lectures in order to take notes or record-
ings that can be utilized in routine Office
mash-ups. Collecting, on the verge of
hoarding, is essential to the Office. (On
the other hand, see §§ 3.2 and 3.5, along
with Appendix 4.5 "Terry Gilliam's Glove
Compartment.")

2   Employees are expected to be mindful
of others, clean up after themselves, and
flush the toilet after each use.

3   While we encourage promiscuous flirta-
tion with both of the major dead ends of
contemporary architectural discourse —
Functional   Positivism   (sustainability,
socioeconomic responsibility) and Formal
Positivism (scripting) — you should probably subscribe to the deep-seated sus-
picion that both of these dead ends, if
allowed to grow into their mature forms

of false positivism and expressionism, are natural enemies of an avant-garde. Positivist techniques producing gestural expressionism are to be avoided. (See Appendix 0 "General Office Protocol" (G.O.P.), included here for reference, and Appendix 6.2 "R. Smithson's East Coast West Coast Part 2," concerning the second film of his trilogy.)

4   The library (books and non-perishable materials) is a resource for the Office. Please take advantage of it, especially in your search for various forms of repetition and rhyme (which are so central to Office production). But do try to keep it neat and orderly. Remember that books are useful for generating arcane footnotes, and the Office is interested in an architecture with footnotes. (See Appendix 3.2 "Learning How To Write like D. F. Wallace.") Reshelve books and materials in their proper location. Please do not remove books from the Office, but feel free to add to the outdated architectural history textbook section of the library with your own materials.

5   The Office is committed to recycling. Please do your part to separate all paper, plastic and metal products, expired

"avant-garde" practices, ink cartridges, obsolete computer equipment, "obsolete" drawing technologies, light bulbs, formal dead-ends, tennis shoes, tires, etc., along with organic forms that are suitable for composting. Bear in mind that even the Russian Constructivists recycled previous material to assemble a self-proclaimed avant-garde. (See Appendix 1.7 "Boym's Off-Modern Reader" and Appendix 4.9 "Max Schier's On Classical vs. Modern Collage.") Make worth of waste.

PART 4
Other Employee Responsibilities

1   You are responsible for your own dishes and for cleaning up any crumbs around work stations which, if left unattended, may cause a recurrence of the Great Ant Swarm Infestation (GASI) of 2004. These swarms are infesting many offices to this day and are to be avoided, unless deemed friendly.

2   You are responsible for nurturing the Office's various self-organizing systems. These include the mold colonies on the compost heap, the software programs on the bio-fuel server farm in the basement, the static electrical phone system,

and the sustainable solar array surrounding the Office headquarters, which may require hourly maintenance to ensure proper functioning.

3   You are responsible for answering the phone. Especially awkward employees may be excused from this task. Please do not hang up on clients unless previously authorized to do so.

4   You should aim to produce architecture which functions like a form of music that sounds right to some and like noise to others. The Office should be thought of as an experimental pop band (See Appendix 7.3 "Rhythmic Dissonance as Protagonist in Contemporary Pop: Black Dice, Autre Ne Veut, Girl Talk, Four Tet, Schizophrenic Lovers, etc.")

5   You are responsible for working within the post-medium condition of our Office. The longstanding rupture between representation and the real (Art / Life) has generated fracturing forces that have fragmented architectural production into a myriad of genres. Multiplying and competing definitions of architectural media now run rampant with strategies based on

geometry, materiality, typology, structure, program, computation, phenomenology, narrative, context, figuration, and performance, to name a few. This speciation of the discipline demonstrates architecture's post-medium condition. Today we have neither a singular disciplinary authenticity nor representational one. (Please refer to sections §§ 3.1 and 3.4 for specific duties related to § 4.5.)

Appendix 6.2
Indifference, Maybe

Our work does not pontificate, it only mumbles, if anything. We're interested in instrumentalizing indifference.

The demise of the architectural discipline through the loss of a clear medium-specificity has disrupted the dominating formalist / structuralist / post-structuralist narrative of the architectural avant-garde and the academy. We have gone from hegemonic resistance in Marxist criticism toward totalizing immersion in the economy or Pierre Bourdieu's "field of cultural production." The unprecedented success of the '60s and '70s is an ongoing oppression of liberation. The baby boomers and "postmodernism" — not the goofy pedimented

76   MOS

buildings or the scatological piles of sticks and beams, but rather the discourse that hollowed out architecture like a hand puppet — has at last exhausted its exhaustion. Those games were once a liberating escape, having produced a clear discipline, an ontology of values. Now we must escape their escape.

If the myth of Modernism was that it operated across multiple registers, multiple disciplines, as a search for an unprecedented unity, and if Postmodernism (not Pomo) was relinquishing the aspiration of utopian unification and instead instrumentalizing fragmentation, then our current moment is something else. Today we are not lamenting the loss of the whole. We are content to occupy parallel ontologies — a simultaneity of multiple subjectivities, foams, niches, networks, perhaps due to the ubiquity of social media, etc. We have been witnessing the genre-fication of architecture in the loss of a clear dominant "style." The demise of the architectural discipline (as suggested in the Supplementary Addendum 23.1B) is due to the loss of a clear consensus about medium-specificity. Medium-specificity is the means through which we produce and critique architecture (for example, orthographic projection, or structure, or program, and so on). Today, even within the realm of disciplinary

autonomy, we have devolved into an archi-
pelago of disparate posturing: the digital
freaks, the nerdy geometers, the automated
techno-utopians, the conceptual ephemer-
alists, the brooding materialists, the autistic
formalists, the slick programmists, humorless
neo-pragmatists, DIY-ers, activist do-gooders,
cartoon hipsters, sustainable opportunists,
etc. Each of these niches, spheres, has their
own enthusiasts, vocabularies, value systems
and utopian desires. We're left to grapple with
a politics produced through aesthetics alone.

Through aesthetics, architecture is rendered
political. This can be illustrated through the
clichéd analogy of architecture as quote
un-quote music that Goethe once wrote and
has since been repeated *ad nauseam*. Music is
the most advanced and sublimated aesthetic
project. Architects, like musicians, produce
momentary subjectivities. Some produce eth-
nic folk tunes or earnest activist work song.
Some prefer rave music, some ambient, some
technical virtuosity; some need lyrics; some
are inclined toward the effects of patterns;
some like grandeur, some noise, etc. Each
genre has its own enthusiasts who care deeply
about the material and feel enfranchised or
liberated by it. For these groups, a particular
music feels more right or more interesting,

and as a result they momentarily believe their music to be better than another. The aesthetic quality of music produces identity and political constituencies — an example of what Rancière identifies as art's ability to "constitute a new collective world" through the production of its own politics (see *The Aesthetic Revolution and Its Outcomes*). Architecture, like music, is ontological. If someone says I listen to _____, we know that it's likely they also wear _____, eat _____, and that their politics are _____. Aesthetics construct identity. They produce one group that says "turn it up" and another that says "that sounds terrible." Though fleeting, such constructed subjectivities suggest that an architecture conceived of like music is momentary, produced only to be eventually replaced.

Techno is the aesthetic equivalent to the Parametric, both dreaming of total control, aiming for an expressionism only achieved through positivist logics and repetition. In our office, we use the same techniques of the Parametric to produce noise and lose control instead of orchestrating the perfect symphony of slick geometries. We're interested in somehow getting it wrong. We use video game engines to produce a world in which design and analysis are collapsed.

The first two illustrations in Eisenman's *Notes on Conceptual Architecture* are Donald Judd and Sol LeWitt. This pair of images sets up a disciplinary space, privileging tactics of geometry in tandem with those of methodology or "following instructions." We imagined a rewriting whereby the text remains the same, but the illustrations change. If we replace Judd and LeWitt with Serra and Smithson, then we could instantly produce an alternate universe, an alternative disciplinary ontology in possession of new subjectivities based on material, mass, weight and entropy.

Instrumentalizing indifference requires disciplinary maps and discursive narratives in order to locate a space in which to work. We use these to form some other frequency, collapsing aesthetic and ontological niches into something that is not a smooth and easy relationship. We're looking for an architecture that operates post-medium. We are not trying to eradicate difference, or to turn everything into a swarm. Architecture exists in an object-narrative relationship, through a sort of ontological flatness. The products of history — techniques, representation, technology — can be mixed, producing new associations, identities, audiences and constituencies. We believe in an architecture that is in conversation with

80   MOS

other architectures. Unification would only depoliticize architecture altogether.

When we say something is beautiful, or elegant, we mean a kind of coherence — a recognizable value, an attempt at stabilizing and unifying value to avoid the risk of discordance. If anything we hope our work will not be unifying. We're OK with being a momentary reprieve for a small group.

■

THE EXPEDITER

FADE IN:

Exterior, MONTY'S, Day. A '60s steakhouse is in a semi-decrepit state on the edge of a major suburban thoroughfare.

> CARY (V.O.)
> A city is like a forest.

> DUTCH (V.O.)
> All right.

Interior, MONTY'S, continuous. Sitting on one side of a dimly lit booth CARY BULLARD, 40 and youthful, leans forward.

> CARY
> It starts off as nothing. Take Yosemite after the last Ice Age. Just raw granite. Then all these species arrive and compete for survival. First the lichens and mosses, then the bushes and shrubs, finally the trees.

DUTCH VANOVER, a distinguished 65, crosses his arms.

> DUTCH
> The trees.

> CARY
> Yeah. They fight for survival until one sort of dominates.

It becomes the dominant species. I mean, there's definitely a bunch of species, but the competition continues until a sort of equilibrium is reached with just the right mix. But the forest is characterized by this dominant species. The lodgepole pine, for instance.

DUTCH
And how is a city like this?

CARY
In cities, development occurs in waves. It has to do with economic, not ecological, cycles, but it's the same principle.

DUTCH
The arrival of species, the competition for dominance ...

CARY
Exactly. Like here in Los Angeles. The first economy revolved around the missions. Which is reflected in the mission architecture. The next economy ...

DUTCH
Cattle?

CARY
Right. And adobe architecture.

DUTCH
Then what, citrus?

CARY
Exactly. When Victorians ruled the earth.

DUTCH
(flatly) Fascinating.

CARY
You think?

Dutch swirls his drink, then downs it.

DUTCH
So where do you see all this going?

CARY

Going?

DUTCH

What do you plan to do with this theory of yours?

CARY

I don't know. It's all in the research phase. I mean, maybe it could be a book. Down the line.

DUTCH

So what is it you need from me?

CARY

Need? I'm not sure ...

DUTCH

You need money, don't you.

CARY

Do I? I think I can maybe get a grant. *(realizing)* Wait, you think I asked you here to get money?

Dutch smiles fondly.

DUTCH

The last time you asked me to lunch I was certain you needed money.

CARY

Yeah, well ...

DUTCH

Imagine my surprise. I usually see things coming from a mile away. You had all the telltale signs of someone sniffing for cash. But no. *(amused, shaking his head)* And what did you want?

CARY

Your daughter's hand.

DUTCH

My daughter's hand. Dammit, that was good! You totally skunked me.

> CARY

See, that's the thing.

> DUTCH

The thing?

> CARY

Now I need you to take it back.

> DUTCH

Take what back?

> CARY

Her hand.

Dutch squints, first confused, then annoyed.

CUT TO:

Exterior, THE DESIGN COUNSEL, Day. Cary runs past a large orange Modernist sculpture to the door of a large black cube, swinging it open.

Interior, THE DESIGN COUNSEL, Continuous. Cary runs into an open architectural studio where several INTERNS, 20s, buzz about a large architectural model, wrapping it.

> CARY

Sorry guys. Lunch with the future father-in-law, couldn't escape.

FARID, 35, well-dressed, smiles wryly.

> FARID

Explains the martini breath.

JASON, 32, wiry, his tie tucked into his shirt, lifts the model.

> JASON

Listen, dude, we've got to get out of here. The Chief is already pissed we haven't submitted yet. If we miss the deadline ...

Cary follows his glance to the corner office. ELLIOTT ROBERTS, 55, stares through the glass at Cary, who jumps to another part of the model.

                         CARY
    I'm on it.

CUT TO:

Exterior, BUILDING DEPARTMENT, Day. Jason and Farid maneuver the model through the front door, which is being held open by Cary.

Interior, BUILDING DEPARTMENT, Continuous. Jason and Farid place the model against the wall. Cary grabs a number. He gets 644. He looks up at the television screen. They're at 573. He sighs.

Interior, BUILDING DEPARTMENT, Later. The number on the screen is 642. Cary's knee bounces nervously, his eyes glued to the screen. Jason and Farid check out the women walking the floor.

                         FARID
    Hi. My name is Farid. Have you met my pet hamster?

                         JASON
    I want to schmeckel you.

Cary checks the screen: 4:25 p.m. A customer leaves the counter. Plan checker, ERNESTO, 45, calls out.

                        ERNESTO
    643. 643? Last call, 643.

Cary looks around. No one is answering. He starts to get up. Suddenly a striking bleached-blonde, PETRA CRUZ, mid-30s, swoops in, a milk crate on wheels filled with rolls of drawings trailing behind her.

                         PETRA
    Ernie, hi. *(slipping into the chair)* I know it's not my turn,
    I just have a quick little thing.

                        ERNESTO
    Petra, it's always your turn.

                         CARY
    (turning to his colleagues) Did you just see that?

                         JASON
    A vanilla milkshake.

FARID
Blonde, smooth, and delicious.

Cary approaches the counter, livid.

CARY
Hey, it was my turn!

ERNESTO
Are you 643?

CARY
644, but she doesn't even have a number.

ERNESTO
Doesn't matter. It's not your turn.

CARY
(frustrated, huffing while sitting) Who does she think she is?

JASON
A sweet honey muffin, that's who.

FARID
A nibble is all I ask.

Petra stands up, leaves, glancing at Cary, smiling.

PETRA
You're up. *(she looks back to the counter)* Thanks, Ernesto.

ERNESTO
Always a pleasure.

Cary drags his drawings as Jason and Farid set the model on the counter.

ERNESTO
Did I call your number?

CARY
No, but we're next.

ERNESTO
We're closed.

CARY
But it's 4:29. We still have one minute.

ERNESTO
Not according to my watch.

CARY
But the screen ...

ERNESTO
(shrugging) Sorry. *(he stands)*

CARY
Oh no. No way. We have to submit this project today or we're totally fucked.

ERNESTO
What can I say? You should have made an appointment. Or at least come in earlier.

CARY
I came in two hours ago. Maybe if you guys worked a little harder...

Ernesto smiles at the insult, walks toward his office behind the counter.

CARY
(almost vibrating with frustration) Look. I know the damned Mayor. Maybe I'll just give him a call.

ERNESTO
(amused, turns back to Cary) That's a great idea. Maybe you can submit your project to him. *(he snickers as he disappears into his office)*

Cary stands open mouthed as his door CLICKS shut. Petra Cruz suddenly appears at Cary's side.

PETRA
It's not who you know, it's who you get.

CARY
What's that supposed to mean?

PETRA
Watch and learn. *(she passes behind the counter and goes to Ernesto's office, tapping gently)* Ernesto?

The door opens and Ernesto's head appears.

ERNESTO
What is it, my dear?

PETRA
There is just one more thing …

The door swings open. Petra casts a knowing smile to Cary before disappearing inside.

CUT TO:

Exterior, THE EDISON, Sunset. A retro bar at the base of a downtown LA office building.

Interior, THE EDISON, Continuous. Camera pans along the bar, stopping at Farid, who is talking up Candace, a 20-something hipster.

FARID
Have you ever been with a guy who giggles during sex?

CANDACE
(furrowing her brow) Can't say that I have.

FARID
Would you like to?

Candace smirks, then turns away. Farid sips his drink, looks around. Cary and Petra are sitting at a booth.

CARY
I think there should be a law that developers who want to demolish a building have to prove to a jury of their peers that what they're putting up is better than what they're tearing down.

PETRA
Ah, yes. The anxiety of the changing city.

                    CARY
Exactly. Wow. I guess I totally misjudged you.

                    PETRA
Just because I know a little critical theory?

                    CARY
No. I don't know. I guess I've never actually met one of you.

                    PETRA
One of who?

                    CARY
An Expediter. I mean, I've always wondered: What do
you guys actually do?

                    PETRA
(pausing for effect) Whatever it takes.

                    CARY
Really? Whatever?

                    PETRA
(smiling flatly) What was that you submitted?

                    CARY
Just this project. For a competition. They want to fix up
the area around the old plaza. Next to Olvera Street.

                    PETRA
Think you have a chance?

                    CARY
Doubtful. Our submission is pretty out there.

                    PETRA
This is LA. How out there can it be?

                    CARY
It's based on this idea: urban succession. You know,
that a city evolves kind of like a forest, with particular
building species dominating during economic expan-
sions. (off her glazed look) You know, so in time, a city
becomes an archive of successive economies?

PETRA
Building species. I like that.

CARY
I know. Pretty crazy. But it kind of makes the city more legible.

Petra, nodding, returns to her drink, taking a long, slow sip. Silent.

CARY
What?

PETRA
(pausing) Nothing.

CARY
No, really. What?

PETRA
It's just ... it's a cute theory.

CARY
Cute? Cute?

PETRA
Well, the whole concept of successionism is retrospective, right; it's a label you put on something after it's happened.

CARY
So?

PETRA
So, wouldn't it be more interesting to look at what's actually happening as it's happening?

CARY
I ... don't even know how you would do that.

PETRA
The problem with you humans is you're species-ist. You're so fascinated with yourselves that you can't see past your own scale.

CARY

You humans? What are you, some sort of alien?

PETRA

When you consider that as a species we are, for the most part, a non-native invasive pest across the globe, I prefer to think of myself — all of us, really — as macrobes, just one of many species interacting within the macrocosm. The byproduct of our interactions is everything we produce — art, music, babies, war — as well as buildings. If the microcosm determines evolution in a forest, the macrocosm handles the next scale up.

CARY

Which is the city.

PETRA

Among other things.

CARY

(considering, then smiling) The metrocosm.

PETRA

Nice. The metrocosm. Which is bigger than the city itself, really. I mean, L.A. extends probably from Camarillo to San Clemente, from Malibu to Yucaipa, a continuous smear of macrobial residue spread across Southern California.

CARY

That's vaguely disgusting.

PETRA

If the evolution of a forest is driven by signaling and exchange occurring in the microcosm, then maybe the evolution of city is driven by interactions within the metrocosm. This would suggest that the city evolves building by building, each of which is the end result of a specific interaction between particular individuals. Which makes the evolution of cities far more granular than your urban successionism would imply.

CARY

If you say so.

Petra leans in, placing her hand on Cary's thigh. Cary pretends not to notice.

PETRA

But maybe it goes even deeper: the interactions that produce each building are between individuals who bring their own vision for a project, right? In more traditional societies there is a tremendous overlap of visions between people, so there's a certain level of agreement to what the built environment should look like. But in a place like L.A., people are coming from all over, so everyone is different, bringing their own mix of cultural influences. If you think of it in terms of successionism, maybe our minds themselves are ecosystems comprising all the various cultures and lessons and traumas we've experienced throughout our lives with one or more dominating our decision making, compelling us to make certain judgments about everything. Which is why we fight for what we want. Let's suppose that an idea for a project is born of an imbalance perceived by whatever mix of cultures currently rules the mind of a politician or developer, whether that imbalance is programmatic or financial. The rest of us come to the project with our own ideas of how best to address that imbalance. Which makes it incredibly important for each of us to weigh in. The fight is key: that interaction — between the client, the architect, the contractor, the building department — that's what really determines the form of our cities. You have to have a point of view and, more important, you have to fight for it, I mean really fight. That would make the opinion the basic unit of force driving the evolution of cities. Think about it: if a forest adjusts to imbalance through communication at the microbial level, the city does so through the clash of individual macrobial opinions on how best to address a perceived imbalance.

Cary just stares at her. Petra leans back, returning to her drink.

CARY

So, what you saying is that it's kind of an ecosystem springing from an egosystem.

PETRA

Bravo. Yes. Exactly.

CARY
(considering) Where did you get all this?

PETRA
I've got a Ph.D. in macrobiology from Caltech. It was sort of my thesis.

CARY
Shouldn't you be working in a lab or something?

PETRA
But, this is my lab.

■

Keith Mitnick

RAINY SEA

Rainy Sea is a small piece of land located in the middle of a large river separating the United States from Canada. Historical accounts of the island are so varied that they appear to refer to entirely different places, and when different maps of the island are overlaid, the shape of their contours seldom agree. Despite its small size, Rainy Sea has played an important role in defining the region by providing an almost comic caricature of the many masquerades, manipulations and political deceptions that have characterized the area's unique history. From a distance, Rainy Sea is abandoned, overgrown with trees and resembles a wilderness.

Though it is located near a large city, Rainy Sea feels isolated and far away. Throughout its history, the island has been repeatedly discovered, built up, torn down and abandoned and is currently littered with the remains of numerous buildings including a prison, an aquarium, a bunker, and a series of small decaying factories. Along with the forests and random wildlife that have grown over the fragments of remaining structures, quarries and a cemetery are

94

the vestiges of an amusement park built many years ago that no one has bothered to remove. Stacks of rusted scaffolding and fallen statues — once used to decorate the park's ticket stands and concessions — now line the crumbling edges of empty swimming pools and dissolving beachfronts, and concrete bunkers once covered by earth stand exposed atop eroding hillsides. The arrangements of roads and trees, lacking the presence of the buildings that once justified them, suggest a strange topography of non-destinations and vacant centers.

The island is a geographical conundrum, a bizarre assembly of familiar things disoriented from their original contexts and randomly inserted back into circumstances to which they no longer relate. More curious than the array of once-purposeful constructions rendered useless is the way they conjoin, fall apart and entice one to draw connections among them, despite the futility of doing so with any certainty. For those who have grown up in the nearby city, the island is more of an idea about a destination than a place they would ever go, something to be seen through rather than thought about. The apparent invisibility of Rainy Sea is what allows it to hide what happens there. From military bases and secret prisons to storage facilities and illegal dumpsites, the island has been a tool for "disappearing" the functions it provides.

■

The sound of the small plane's engine was the only indication of its presence as it flew through the early morning fog. Paul stared into a cloudy window while an overweight steward wheeled a service cart down

95

the aisle along mostly empty seats. As the steward neared the back of the plane, Paul imagined the air-craft's overloaded tail push the plane's nose involun-tarily upward — and was reminded of a painting he had seen of a tortured saint looking up to heaven as a swarm of demons carried his body off to hell.

Paul had wanted to stay on the island for the sake of his sisters, but ran away to protect himself. At first he judged himself a failure for having abandoned them, and then later for continuing to doubt the right-ness of his decision. As his sense of inadequacy grew, so too did the need to invent the possibility of a different future for himself. He visualized the embryo of another "Paul" in the form of a minute sub-frac-tion of himself he called the "precious pearl." The pearl fed upon his anxieties like a friendly parasite and converted them into growth food for the second body that, he hoped, would one day replace him. As he awaited the insurrection of the growing pearl, the old Paul rehearsed dialog for the Nuremberg-like war trials in which the unsupportive parts of his former self would be tried and hung.

Returning to the island now after so many years, Paul realized that his faith in the pearl had waned, and the image he had clung to of it glowing deep inside had faded. And though the idea of a better Paul growing out of the person he was no longer inspired him, the question remained as to whether his sense of something missing was the bodily sensation of an unoccupied area allocated for a fully grown pearl, or if the story of the precious-pearl itself had infected his otherwise fulfill-able life with the idea of an irrep-arable hole.

■

I grew up in a single house within two families. My parents each lived there with my twin sisters, Agnes and Paula, and I, but on different days of the week. My mother was there from Sunday to Wednesday. She was moody and demanding and managed to convince us that her needs were more always important than ours. My memories of my father are less distinct. He was with us Thursday to Saturday, seldom spoke and drifted aimlessly through the house like a ghost. My mother obliterated us with her presence, and my father hardly appeared at all. The two of them rotated in and out of the house while we shuttled between their lives.

As children, my sisters and I each had some identifiable problem with vision. I wore bifocal glasses that quadrupled my view, and Agnes had an eye patch that cut hers in half. Paula had a stigmatism in her left eye that caused her sight to double and blur. The eye doctor told me that one of my eyes was lazy — it didn't want to do its job, drifted inward and left its partner to do all of the work. I liked the idea that there was confusion within my effort to see and politics among my parts. I had to wear thick glasses that made a horizontal line across my eyes where the seams of the differing lenses met. It was strange to me that the intersection of transparent things would produce visible edges. My glasses were frequently dirty, though I seldom noticed until I was reminded by others to clean them.

■

Paul gasped in his seat as the small dot came into view through the tiny window and then grew into an island as the plane descended. If he had known

97

the night before that he would be on a flight back to Rainy Sea the next day, he would have found a way to avoid it, but there he was returning to a place he wanted nothing more than to forget. As the wheels of the plane touched down, racing Paul towards his own distant past, the edges of the island reached up around him like a rising abyss. He rushed through the airport, kept his head down, and did what he could to block out the familiarity of the place. He renewed self-promises to leave the following day and struggled against his body's efforts to re-root itself in the place from which it had so long ago been extracted. The image of a locomotive speeding towards disaster appeared in Paul's head like *The Little Engine That Could* — but in place of the reassuring mantra of "I think I can, I think I can" he recalled from the book, he heard "fuck, fuck, fuck, fuck".

■

My mother was the captain of a ferryboat that crossed back and forth between the island and the nearby city. She worked long hours that required us to ride along on the boat whenever we wanted to spend time with her. The highlights of these trips were the conversations we had about river navigation. I was fascinated to discover that the negotiation of local waterways had nothing to do with what one saw with their eyes and everything to do with their knowledge of the unseen shape of the river bottom below.

My father was a librarian who was more interested in books than life. No matter where he was, he was reading. He walled himself away in stories to avoid dealing with the world. Over and over, I tried to talk to him by telling him things about my life as

UP

though I was a character in one of his favorite books, switching in and out of different voices to disguise my need for his attention in the perspective of different literary characters. "It's so BRIGHT in here," I would shout as the Invisible Man. "Why can't you SEE me?"

■

Paul drove off in a cab without telling the driver where to go. When the phone had awoken him the night before, a man told him that one of his sisters was in the hospital and the other had disappeared. The man asked if Paul knew where a mysterious suitcase that his sister had asked for was and insisted that he come to the island as soon as possible. As the taxi sped forward, Paul considered options: he could go to Paula, look for Agnes, or visit the house where he had grown up and Paula still lived. Sitting in the seat not deciding, he erased everything he saw by re-describing it to himself: "That's not the place where anything I can remember ever happened."

He thought about the suitcase his mother had held against her chest every day as she rocked on the edge of the couch. The impression she left on the cushion remained for many years after her death and distracted him from ever wondering about the suitcase — though, thinking back, Paul wondered why he hadn't been more curious. As the taxi turned suddenly to avoid an exposed manhole, one of its wheels slipped into it. The driver accelerated to free the spinning wheel as Paul lurched into the back of his seat, hearing, but not responding to, the driver's demand that he get out of the car. With the sound of metal grinding against pavement, Paul looked up to see a sailboat passing on a trailer, reminding him of

99

the submerged dry dock where they kept his mother's ferry after the crash.

■

Our house stood between the edges of a forest and the river on the north end of Rainy Sea. Its windows were arranged in a way that, looking out, one had the impression of being in a large unmoving ship aimed permanently upstream. In my memory, the house is comprised of a series of fragmented hallways and incomplete rooms, each separated by inaccessible pockets of empty space and furnished in half-measures that made it difficult to know how to use the rooms despite the obvious purposes they were intended to serve. Thinking back, I have trouble reconciling what I know about the location of the house with what I remember seeing out of its windows. It is never clear to me if the house has shaped my memories, or if my memories have simply constructed a sympathetic landscape in which to appear.

Among the few pieces of advice my father ever gave me was "make yourself invisible and follow the rules." My mother's philosophy was the opposite — she thought rules were for other people and that we should do whatever we wanted, as long as we didn't get in her way. I would have preferred the voice of a single all-knowing authority to the mutually exclusive set of life lessons I received from them, regardless of what it told me, or so I believed. Our house corroborated the madness of our conflicted parenting perfectly, comprised as it was of a series of maze-like rooms that repeated and divided, concealed some areas and falsified the limits of others. It had everything a house is supposed to have, but in the wrong

100

number and arrangement, like a backwards head with two brains and a giant eye.

■

The tradition of making Rainy Sea appear different than it was extends back to the origin of its name. Similar to Iceland — a name devised by Icelanders to keep foreigners away by making it sound less appealing than it was — the Canadians named the island Rien Ici, French for "nothing here." To the Americans, who would eventually steal it by changing "Rien Ici" into "Rainy Sea," the mispronunciation was a way to alter its history. By calling the island "Canadian" during American prohibition, Americans were able to sell illegal alcohol legally, and when Canadians needed to dispose of the garbage they didn't allow in their own country, the island became "American". When American businesses stood to gain more from Canadian tax laws than their own, they happily ceded the nationality of the place to the other, and when it benefited both countries to have a place to incarcerate political prisoners free of their respective laws, it was deemed a no-man's land.

■

Made Up Symposium
Photo Catherine R.
Wygal + Deanna McClure

Contributors

■ JULIAN BLEECKER (PhD) is an engineer, designer, photographer and co-founder of OMATA. He also founded the design-technology studio Near Future Laboratory while a professor at the University of Southern California's School of Cinematic Arts. He worked as a design-technologist at Nokia's Advanced Design Studio and has a BS in Electrical Engineering from Cornell and an MS in computer-human interaction from the University of Washington. He earned his PhD from the University of California, Santa Cruz where his doctoral dissertation focused on science, fiction, technology, and culture.
□ nearfuturelaboratory.com

■ BENJAMIN H. BRATTON is a theorist whose work spans philosophy, art, and design. He is Associate Professor of Visual Arts and Director of D:GP, The Center for Design and Geopolitics at the University of California, San Diego. His research is situated at the intersections of contemporary social and political theory, computational media and infrastructure, architectural and urban design problems, and the politics of synthetic ecologies and biologies. Current work focuses on the political geography of cloud computing, massively-granular universal addressing systems, and alternate models of ecological governance. His book, *The Stack: On Software and Sovereignty*, was published by MIT Press.

Most recent selected texts include: "What We Do is Secrete: On Virilio, Planetarity and Data Visualization," "Geoscapes & the Google Caliphate: On Mumbai Attacks," "Root the Earth: On Peak Oil Apohenia," and "Suspicious Images / Latent Interfaces" with Natalie Jeremijenko.

Bratton is a frequent advisor and consultant to public and private organizations. He is currently a Fellow with Lybba, an open-data healthcare design nonprofit. In a previous life, he was the Director of the Advanced Strategies Group at Yahoo!
□ bratton.info

■ EMMET BYRNE is the Design Director of the Walker Art Center. He also helps edit and design a sporadic magazine called *Task Newsletter*, with Jon Sueda and Alex DeArmond.
□ walkerart.org

■ STUART CANDY is Associate Professor in the School of Design at Carnegie Mellon University, Director of Situation Lab, and a Fellow of The Long Now Foundation and the Museum of Tomorrow. He is a pioneer of practices using design, games, performance and transmedia storytelling to bring futures to life, and so amplify the foresight capacity of individuals, organisations, and communities. Dr. Candy has developed and introduced experiential futures / design fiction techniques to practitioners and audiences around the world, and his collaborative projects have appeared in numerous contexts from museums to magazines, festivals, campuses, conferences, and city streets. He blogs at The Sceptical Futuryst, and can be contacted at *stuart@ futuryst.com*
□ futuryst.com

■ Dunne & Raby use design as a medium to stimulate discussion and debate amongst designers, industry, and the public about the social, cultural, and ethical implications of existing and emerging technology. At The New School they are experimenting with research and teaching platforms that use design as a catalyst for a form of interdisciplinary imagining that synthesizes social and political thought, world-making, and emerging technology — a sort of 'many worlds lab' dedicated to sustaining the idea of multiple possibilities in the face of an increasingly monolithic worldview of our technological future.

Their publications include *Hertzian Tales* (1999, 2005), *Design Noir* (2001), and *Speculative Everything* (2013, Japanese version 2015). Projects include *Technological Dream Series, No 1: Robots* (2007), *Designs For An Over Populated Planet: Foragers* (2010), *The United Micro Kingdoms* (2013), and *The School of Constructed Realities* (2015).

Dunne & Raby's work has been exhibited at MoMA in New York, the Pompidou Centre in Paris, and the Design Museum in London, and is in several permanent collections including MoMA, the Victoria and Albert Museum, and the Austrian Museum of Applied Arts.

FIONA RABY is Professor of Design and Emerging Technology at Parsons, The New School for Design, and a Fellow at the Graduate Institute for Design, Ethnography & Social Thought at The New School for Social Research (NSSR). From 2011–16 she was professor of Industrial Design (id2) at the University of Applied Arts in Vienna, She has taught Architecture (ads04), Computer Related Design and Design Interactions at The Royal College of Art since 1995 and she was reader in Design Interactions between 2005 and 2015.

☐ dunneandraby.co.uk

■ TIM DURFEE heads Tim Durfee Studio in Los Angeles. After earning his architecture degree from Yale, Durfee moved to LA to teach architec-tural design and direct the Visual Studies program at the Southern California Institute of Architecture. Eventually, he reoriented his work toward an expanded interdisciplinary practice at the intersection of architecture, art, and media. Since 2010, Durfee has been professor at ArtCenter College of Design's Media Design Practices program, a department focusing on emerging roles and contexts for design and technology.

Durfee's independent and collaborative work has won awards and distinctions from the AIA, AIGA, *Print*, *Build*, and Architizer. In 2015, Tim was chosen to be included as one of Fifty Under Fifty: Innovators of the 21st Century, by jury Stanley Tigerman, Jeanne Gang, Qingyun Ma, and Marion Weiss.

His work has been published and exhibited widely. Among the exhibitions he has curated is *Made Up: Design's Fictions*, which featured 40 international designers and included Durfee's *The Rather Large Array* (granted the AIA | LA Honor award for architecture in 2012.) In 2015 he co-curated *Now, There: Scenes from the Post-Geographic City*, which received the Bronze Dragon at the UABB

Biennale in Shenzhen. TD dedicates this book, with love, to his storytelling father.

☐ timdurfee.com

■ SAM JACOB is principal of Sam Jacob Studio for architecture and design, a practice whose work spans scales and disciplines from urban design through architecture, design, art and curatorial projects. He has worked internationally on award-winning projects and has exhibited at major museums such as the V&A, MAK, and The Art Institute of Chicago as well as cultural events including the Venice Architecture Biennale. He is Professor of Architecture at UIC, Chicago, visiting professor at Yale School of Architecture, Director of Night School at the Architectural Association, and columnist for Art Review and Dezeen. Previously he was a founding director of FAT Architecture.

☐ samjacob.com

■ PETER LUNENFELD is a professor in the Design | Media Arts department at UCLA. He is one of the steering committee members of the campus-wide, interdisciplinary Digital Humanities undergraduate minor and graduate concentration. He has a B.A. in history from Columbia University, an M.A. in Media Studies from SUNY Buffalo, and a Ph.D. from UCLA in Film, Television and New Media from UCLA.

His current research

interests are taking him deeper into questions about new modes of knowledge formation that go beyond print, the design of the digital humanities, and the centrality of meaning making to digital culture. He has held fellowships at the Columbia University Institute for Scholars at Reid Hall in Paris, and in the Vectors program at the USC Annenberg Center.
☐ peterlunenfeld.com

■ GEOFF MANAUGH is author of the *New York Times*-bestselling book *A Burglar's Guide to the City*, about the relationship between burglary and architecture, as well as the critically acclaimed website BLDGBLOG. He has written for *The New Yorker*, *New Scientist*, *Domus*, and *The New York Times Magazine*, among many other publications, and he has curated exhibitions at the Nevada Museum of Art and Storefront for Art and Architecture. Manaugh is also the former director of Studio-X NYC at the Columbia University Graduate School of Architecture, Planning, and Preservation.
☐ bldgblog.com

■ After earning architecture degrees from UC Berkeley and Yale, TOM MARBLE worked for firms as diverse as SOM and Morphosis, Chermayeff & Geismar, and The Irvine Company. Since 2001, his practice, Marbletecture, has

divided its time between designing buildings, writing about cities, and teaching, which he has done at USC, Woodbury University, Colorado College, and SCI-Arc. Tom Marble's work has appeared in *The Architect's Newspaper*, *MONU Magazine*, *LA Times Magazine*, and *Metropolis*; his pamphlet, *After the city, this (is how we live)* was published by the Los Angeles Forum for Architecture & Urban Design in 2008. Tom is now at work on *The Expediter*, an urban noir following the unfolding drama of a doomed real estate development in downtown Los Angeles.
☐ tommarble.com

■ M-A-U-S-E-R is a collaborative studio, established by Asli Serbest and Mona Mahall in 2007, to reflect and produce architecture in and through different media. Their projects include exhibitions, installations, stage and set designs, as well as video-texts, concepts, and publications, all of them showing enthusiasm for strange online and offline spaces, anti and rational modes of work, and fragmentary forms. Their aim is to negotiate the evolving relationship between architecture, art, and media society. m-a-u-s-e-r's teaching and research strongly resonates with their practice.

They exhibit and publish internationally, among other venues at the Istanbul

Design Biennial (2016), Shenzhen Bi-City Biennale of Urbanism / Architecture (2015), ArtCenter College of Design in Pasadena (2015), Storefront for Art and Architecture in New York (2014, 2015), Biennale di Venezia (2012, 2014), Vancouver Art Gallery (2013), Künstlerhaus Stuttgart (2013), HKW in Berlin (2012), New Museum in New York (2009); in *e-flux* journal, *Volume* magazine, *Perspecta*, *The Gradient* blog of the Walker Art Center, *AArchitecture*, *Deutschlandfunk* and other venues.

They are co-authors of a book on the speculative character of modern architecture — *How Architecture Learned to Speculate* (2009), with Mona Mahall — and editors of *Junk Jet* (since 2007), an independent magazine on architecture, art, and media. They have taught as professors of Foundations of Design and Experimental Architecture at the Stuttgart State Academy of Art and Design. Currently they serve as (visiting) professors of Architecture at Cornell University and of Spatial Dynamics at Rhode Island School of Design.
☐ m-a-u-s-e-r.net

■ Founded by Vinca Kruk and Daniel van der Velden in 2007 as a design and research studio, METAHAVEN has come to define a new methodology in graphic design. The studio's speculative practice privileges the vocabulary of graphic design as a means of knowledge production, using it as a tool to analyze organizational models and power structures. Investigating political and economic design — including nation branding and logo production — in relation to statehood, currency, and information networks, Metahaven places particular emphasis on transparency and visibility.

The Amsterdam-based studio produces a continuous stream of research that rarely results in finite, codified work. They publish books and essays, organize conferences, and collaborate with policymakers, concurrently working on new commissions while maintaining a variety of self-initiated projects. Recent activities have included a range of research, identity and product design for WikiLeaks, as well as proposals for the identity of Sealand, a self-proclaimed sovereign nation-state located on a platform built by the British seven miles off the English coast as part of a naval defense strategy during World War II.
☐ metahaven.net

■ KEITH MITNICK is a principal of Mitnick Roddier, a collaborative design practice founded with Mireille Roddier. Their built work has received numerous awards, including the Young Architects Forum award from the Architectural

League of New York and the Design Vanguard Award from Architectural record Magazine. They have constructed installations in France and the United States at the Chaumont-Sur-Loire International Garden Festival, the Montpellier Festival of Architecture, and the Los Angeles Forum for Architecture + Urbanism. Both Mitnick and Roddier are Associate Professors at the University of Michigan. Mitnick's first book, *Artificial Light*, was published by Princeton Architectural Press in 2008, and he is currently working on a sec-ond book titled *Rainy Sea Architecture*.
☐ mitnick-roddier.com

■ MOS Architects is a New York-based architecture studio, founded by principals Hilary Sample and Michael Meredith in 2003. An internationally recognized architecture practice, MOS was the recipient of the 2015 Cooper Hewitt, Smithsonian Design Museum National Design Award in Architecture, the 2010 American Academy of Arts and Letters Architecture Award, and the 2008 Architectural League of New York Emerging Voices Award. Individual works have similarly received numerous awards and distinctions, most notably: the 2015 Global Holcim Award for sustainable construction (Asia-Pacific Region), for Community Center No. 3 (Lali Gurans Orphanage); the cover of *Abitare* and

an AIA NY State Award of Excellence, for School No. 1 (Krabbesholm Højskole); the 2014 accession of both the firm's modular, off-grid House No. 5 (Museum of Outdoor Arts Element House) into The Museum of Modern Art, Architecture and Design Collection; the acquisition of House No. 3 (Lot No. 6 / Ordos) into the permanent collection of The Art Institute of Chicago; and the selection of Pavilion No. 4 (Afterparty) for the 2009 MoMA PS1 Young Architects Program. Recent work includes: Store No. 2 (Chamber) in Chelsea, NYC; House No. 10, currently under-construction; School No. 2, a competition proposal for the Institute for Advanced Study Commons Building; and Housing No. 4 (Dequindre Cut, Detroit).

Recent and forthcoming publications, both products of and surveys on MOS's work, include *Everything All at Once: The Software, Film, and Architecture of MOS* (Princeton Architectural Press, 2013); MOS: Selected Works (Princeton Architectural Press, 2016); *El Croquis* No. 184 (El Croquis, 2016); *A Situation Constructed From Loose and Overlapping Social and Architectural Aggregates* (AADR, 2016); *An Incomplete Encyclopedia of Scale Figures Without Architecture* (GSAPP Books, 2016); and an *A+U* monograph (forthcoming, 2017).
☐ mos-office.net

UP

MADE

■ SUSANNAH SCHOUWEILER is a writer, editor, and museum wonk. For 12 years, she was Editor-in-Chief of MN Artists at the Walker Art Center and responsible for publication of original arts writing on the homepage, blog, and social media assets. She served as Editor of *Ruminator* magazine, a nationally-distributed art and literature publication. She has written on the arts for a number of regional and national outlets, including *Hyperallergic*, *Rain Taxi Review of Books*, MinnPost, *The Growler*, *Public Art Review*, and the John S. and James L. Knight Foundation's *Knight Arts* blog.

■ BRUCE STERLING is an Austin-born (April 14th 1954) science fiction writer and Net critic, internationally recognized as a cyberspace theorist who is also still based there. However, as a child he also spent a lot of time in India, which can partly explain why today still Sterling is fond of Bollywood movies. Sterling studied journalism. He published his first book, *Involution Ocean*, in 1977. However, he first started becoming famous in Austin by organizing every year a Christmas party where he would present dig-ital art. In the 80s Sterling published *Cheap Truth*, a series of fanzines which are magazines for fans of a particular performer, group, or form of entertainment. He did so under the surprising but revealing pen name of Vincent Omniaveritas. In latin, *vincit omnia veritas* means 'truth conquers all things'. Sterling's writings have been very influential in the cyberpunk movement in literature, specifically

the novels *Heavy Weather* (1994), *Islands in the Net* (1988), *Schismatrix* (1985), and *The Artificial Kid* (1980).
Bruce Sterling's novels include: *Intuition Ocean* (1977), *The Artificial Kid* (1980), *Heavy Weather* (1994), *Holy Fire* (1996), *Distraction* (1998), *Zeitgeist* (2000), *The Zenith Angle* (2004), *Kiosk* (2007), and *The Caryatids* (2009). His essay collection and non-fiction books include *The Hacker Crackdown: Law and Order on the Electronic Frontier* (1993), *Tomorrow Now: Envisioning the Next Fifty Years* (2002), and *Shaping Things* (2005).

■ MIMI ZEIGER is a Los Angeles-based critic, editor, and curator.
Her work is situated at the intersection of architecture and media cultures.
☐ mimizeiger.com

■ We'd like to acknowledge the following practices who contributed to an earlier conception of the publication:

Alice Haldenwang, Laura Couto Rosado, and Tingting Zhang; Alex Lehnerer, Jared Macken, Jayne Kelley, and Lorenzo Stieger; Alexandra Daisy Ginsberg, Sascha Pohflepp, and Andrew Stellitano; AMID.cero9, Andrew Nagata, Captains of Industry, Darryl Chen + Liam Young, David Leonard, Eames Demetrios, Dunne & Raby, Fred Scharmen, Guy Horton, Harrison Atelier, Heather Peterson, Höweler + Yoon Architecture, Ilona Gaynor, Janet Sarbanes, Janette Kim and Eric Carver, Jessica Charlesworth, Jimenez Lai, John Ryan, Keith Krumwiede, Kjen Wilkens, KM & ÉM, Lauren McCarthy, Mark Shepard, Michael Kontopoulos and Jerod Rivera, Neil Denari, Nelly Ben Hayoun Studio, Nicolas Nova, Nitipak Samsen and Wuttin Chansataboot, Paul Preissner with Jesus Corral, John Dillon, Ryan Hernandez, and Erin Patterson; R&Sie(n), Sarah Needham, smudge studio and DodoLab, The Extrapolation Factory, Tanner Teale, Terreform ONE, Urban Operations, William Frohn, and Xefirotarch.